GOD IS THE GOSPEL

GOD
IS THE
GOSPEL

MEDITATIONS ON GOD'S LOVE
AS THE GIFT OF HIMSELF

JOHN PIPER

CROSSWAY

WHEATON, ILLINOIS

Cover design: Patrick Mahoney of The Mahoney Design Team

First printing 2005

Trade paperback edition with new cover 2011

Printed in the United States of America

Trade paperback ISBN: 978-1-4335-2049-5

Library of Congress Cataloging-in-Publication Data

Piper, John, 1946–
   God is the gospel : meditations on God's love as the gift of himself / John Piper.
     p. cm.
   Includes indexes.
   ISBN 13:978-1-58134-751-7
   ISBN 10: 1-58134-751-0 (hc : alk. paper)
    1. God—Love. I. Title.
BT140.P52   2005
231'.6—dc22
                                  2005014843

to
Abraham and Molly Piper
who together are making
marriage and music
for love's best Gift.

From you our life arrives
And into you departs.
Then we begin to live.
You are the life of lives.
You are the heart of hearts.
You are the gift you give.

acp

CONTENTS

A Word of Thanks

First, I say to Jesus Christ, "I thank you that you have answered me and have become my salvation. . . . I have looked upon you in the sanctuary, beholding your power and glory. Because your steadfast love is better than life, my lips will praise you" (Psalm 118:21; 63:2-3).

Second, I say to Noël and Talitha, thank you for loving me as I disappeared to my study for the long days of writing. Thank you for living the gospel with me.

Third, to my prayer support team, thank you for your daily intercession and for doing battle on my behalf against Satan and sin and sickness and sabotage. In his mercy God answered.

Fourth, to the staff and elders of Bethlehem Baptist Church, thank you for the writing leave and for the sacrifices you make for the vision of spreading a passion for the supremacy of God in all things, especially the gospel.

Fifth, to Justin Taylor and Carol Steinbach at Desiring God, thank you for theological sharpening, editing acumen, and cheerful drudgery (the indexes), in addition to fruitful partnership in exalting the truth that God is most glorified in us when we are most satisfied in him.

Finally, to Jonathan Edwards and John Owen whose vision of the glories of Christ has been for my soul a beam of spiritual light and life, thank you.

*Christ also suffered once for sins,
the righteous for the unrighteous,
that he might bring us to God.*

1 PETER 3:18

INTRODUCTION:
WHAT THE WORLD NEEDS
MOST—THE GOSPEL'S
GREATEST GIFT, GOD

Today—as in every generation—it is stunning to watch the shift away from God as the all-satisfying gift of God's love. It is stunning how seldom God himself is proclaimed as the greatest gift of the gospel. But the Bible teaches that the best and final gift of God's love is the enjoyment of God's beauty. "One thing have I asked of the LORD, that will I seek after: that I may dwell in the house of the LORD all the days of my life, to gaze upon the beauty of the LORD and to inquire in his temple" (Ps. 27:4). The best and final gift of the gospel is that we gain Christ. "I count everything as loss because of the surpassing worth of knowing Christ Jesus my Lord. For his sake I have suffered the loss of all things and count them as rubbish, in order that I may gain Christ" (Phil. 3:8). This is the all-encompassing gift of God's love through the gospel—to see and savor the glory of Christ forever.

In place of this, we have turned the love of God and the gospel of Christ into a divine endorsement of our delight in many lesser things, especially the delight in our being made much of. The acid test of biblical God-centeredness—and faithfulness to the gospel—is this: Do you feel more loved because God makes much of you, or because, at the cost of his Son, he enables you to enjoy making much of him forever? Does your happiness hang on seeing the cross of Christ as a witness to your worth, or as a way to enjoy God's worth forever? Is God's glory in Christ the foundation of your gladness?

From the first sin in the Garden of Eden to the final judgment of the great white throne, human beings will continue to embrace the love of God as the gift of everything but himself. Indeed there are ten thousand gifts that flow from the love of God. The gospel of Christ proclaims the news that he has purchased by his death ten thousand blessings for his bride. But none of these gifts will lead to final joy if they have not first led to God. And not one gospel blessing will be enjoyed by anyone for whom the gospel's greatest gift was not the Lord himself.

IS DIVINE LOVE THE ENDORSEMENT OF SELF-ADMIRATION?

The sad thing is that a radically man-centered view of love permeates our culture and our churches. From the time they can toddle we teach our children that feeling loved means feeling made much of. We have built whole educational philosophies around this view of love—curricula, parenting skills, motivational strategies, therapeutic models, and selling techniques. Most modern people can scarcely imagine an alternative understanding of feeling loved other than feeling made much of. If you don't make much of me you are not loving me.

But when you apply this definition of love to God, it weakens his worth, undermines his goodness, and steals our final satisfaction. If the enjoyment of God himself is not the final and best gift of love, then God is not the greatest treasure, his self-giving is not the highest mercy, the gospel is not the good news that sinners may enjoy their Maker, Christ did not suffer to bring us to God, and our souls must look beyond him for satisfaction.

This distortion of divine love into an endorsement of self-admiration is subtle. It creeps into our most religious acts. We claim to be praising God because of his love for us. But if his love for us is at bottom his making much of us, who is really being praised? We are willing to be God-centered, it seems, as long as God is man-centered. We are willing to boast in the cross as long as the cross is a witness to our worth. Who then *is* our pride and joy?[1]

GREAT SELF OR GREAT SPLENDOR?

Our fatal error is believing that wanting to be happy means wanting to be made much of. It feels so good to be affirmed. But the good feeling may be rooted in the worth of self, not the worth of God. This path to happiness is an illusion. And there are clues. There are clues in every human heart even before conversion to Christ. One of those clues is that no one goes to the Grand Canyon or to the Alps to increase his self-esteem. That is not what happens in front of massive deeps and majestic heights. But we do go there, and we go for joy. How can that be, if being made much of is the center of our health and happiness? The answer is that it is not the center. In wonderful moments of illumination there is a witness in our hearts: soul-health and great happiness come not from beholding a great self but a great splendor.

THE HIGHEST, BEST, FINAL, DECISIVE GOOD IN THE GOSPEL

The gospel of Jesus Christ reveals what that splendor is. Paul calls it "the light of the gospel of the glory of Christ, who is the image of God" (2 Cor. 4:4). Two verses later he calls it "the glory of God in the face of Jesus Christ."

When I say that *God Is the Gospel* I mean that the highest, best, final, decisive good of the gospel, without which no other gifts would be good, is the glory of God in the face of Christ revealed for our everlasting enjoyment. The saving love of God is God's commitment to do everything necessary to enthrall us with what is most deeply and durably satisfying, namely himself. Since we are sinners and have no

---

[1] I will deal with the question of proper joy in God's gifts, including people, in Chapter Ten. For now consider, for example, that when Paul says in 1 Thessalonians 2:19, "For what is our hope or joy or crown of boasting before our Lord Jesus at his coming? Is it not you?" the question still remains: What is the ultimate source or ground or bottom or goal of his joy? There is no dispute that people bring us joy. There is no dispute that our own clear conscience is a source of joy (Rom. 14:22). The question is: How does this joy relate to God? Are these things a cause of joy because they show us more of him or lead us toward him? Or is he a joy because he leads us to them?

right and no desire to be enthralled with God, therefore God's love enacted a plan of redemption to provide that right and that desire. The supreme demonstration of God's love was the sending of his Son to die for our sins and to rise again so that sinners might have the right to approach God and might have the pleasure of his presence forever.

In order for the Christian gospel to be good news it must provide an all-satisfying and eternal gift that undeserving sinners can receive and enjoy. For that to be true, the gift must be three things. First, the gift must be purchased by the blood and righteousness of Jesus Christ, the Son of God. Our sins must be covered, and the wrath of God against us must be removed, and Christ's righteousness must be imputed to us. Second, the gift must be free and not earned. There would be no good news if we had to merit the gift of the gospel. Third, the gift must be God himself, above all his other gifts.

It would be a misunderstanding of this book if it were seen as minimizing the battles being fought for a biblical understanding of the *ways and means* God has used in the accomplishment and application of redemption.[2] The fact that this book is focusing on the infinite value of the ultimate goal of the gospel should increase, rather than decrease, our commitment not to compromise the great gospel means God used to get us there.

The gospel is the good news of our final and full enjoyment of the glory of God in the face of Christ. That this enjoyment had to be purchased for sinners at the cost of Christ's life makes his glory shine all the more brightly. And that this enjoyment is a free and unmerited gift makes it shine more brightly still. But the price Jesus paid for the gift and the unmerited freedom of the gift are not the gift. The gift is Christ himself as the glorious image of God—seen and savored with everlasting joy.

---

[2] Another way to say this is that *all* of John Murray's classic statement on *Redemption—Accomplished and Applied* (Grand Rapids, Mich.: Eerdmans, 1955), is crucial, not just the concluding section on "glorification." Our views of the necessity, nature, perfection, and extent of the atonement, and our views of effectual calling, regeneration, faith, repentance, justification, adoption, sanctification, perseverance, and union with Christ are crucial. Nothing I say in this book should be construed to minimize these essential biblical truths. If anything, I hope the preciousness of the goal (seeing and savoring God himself) will make us more vigilant to preserve the truth of the means.

WOULD YOU BE HAPPY IN HEAVEN IF CHRIST WERE NOT THERE?

The critical question for our generation—and for every generation—is this: If you could have heaven, with no sickness, and with all the friends you ever had on earth, and all the food you ever liked, and all the leisure activities you ever enjoyed, and all the natural beauties you ever saw, all the physical pleasures you ever tasted, and no human conflict or any natural disasters, could you be satisfied with heaven, if Christ were not there?

And the question for Christian leaders is: Do we preach and teach and lead in such a way that people are prepared to hear that question and answer with a resounding *No*? How do we understand the gospel and the love of God? Have we shifted with the world from God's love as the gift of himself to God's love as the gift of a mirror in which we like what we see? Have we presented the gospel in such a way that the gift of the glory of God in the face of Christ is marginal rather than central and ultimate? If so, I pray that this book might be one way God wakens us to see the supreme value and importance of "the light of the gospel of the glory of Christ, who is the image of God." I pray that our ministries would have the same focal point as the ministry of John Owen, the great Puritan writer of the seventeenth century. Richard Daniels said of him:

> There is one motif so important to John Owen, so often and so broadly cited by him, that the writer would go so far as to call it the focal point of Owen's theology . . . namely, the doctrine that in the gospel we behold, by the Christ-given Holy Spirit, the glory of God "in the face of Christ" and are thereby changed into his image.[3]

ARE WE PREPARING PEOPLE FOR HEAVEN?

Can we really say that our people are being prepared for heaven where Christ himself, not his gifts, will be the supreme pleasure? And if our people are unfit for that, will they even go there? Is not

---

[3] Richard Daniels, *The Christology of John Owen* (Grand Rapids, Mich.: Reformation Heritage Books, 2004), 92.

the faith that takes us to heaven the foretaste of the feast of Christ? J. C. Ryle once preached a sermon called "Christ Is All" based on Colossians 3:11. In it he said:

> But alas, how little fit for heaven are many who talk of 'going to heaven' when they die, while they manifestly have no saving faith, and no real acquaintance with Christ. You give Christ no honor here. You have no communion with Him. You do not love Him. Alas! what could you do in heaven? It would be no place for you. Its joys would be no joys for you. Its happiness would be a happiness into which you could not enter. Its employments would be a weariness and burden to your heart. Oh, repent and change before it be too late![4]

Nothing fits a person to be more useful on earth than to be more ready for heaven. This is true because readiness for heaven means taking pleasure in beholding the Lord Jesus, and beholding the glory of the Lord means being changed into his likeness (2 Cor. 3:18). Nothing would bless this world more than more people who are more like Christ. For in likeness to Christ the world might see Christ.

WHAT THE WORLD NEEDS MOST

When we celebrate the gospel of Christ and the love of God, and when we lift up the gift of salvation, let us do it in such a way that people will see through it to God himself. May those who hear the gospel from our lips know that salvation is the blood-bought gift of seeing and savoring the glory of Christ. May they believe and say, "Christ is all!" Or, to use the words of the psalmist, "May those who love your salvation say evermore, 'God is great!'" (Ps. 70:4). Not mainly, "Salvation is great," but "God is great!"

May the church of Jesus Christ say with increasing intensity, "The LORD is my chosen portion and my cup" (Ps. 16:5). "As a deer pants for flowing streams, so pants my soul for you, O God. My soul thirsts for God, for the living God" (Ps. 42:1). "We would

---

[4] J. C. Ryle in a sermon titled "Christ is All," from Colossians 3:11. *Holiness: Its Nature, Hindrances, Difficulties, and Roots* (1877; reprint, Moscow, Ida.: Charles Nolan Publishers, 2001), 384.

rather be away from the body and at home with the Lord" (2 Cor. 5:8). "My desire is to depart and be with Christ, for that is far better" (Phil. 1:23).

The world needs nothing more than to see the worth of Christ in the work and words of his God-besotted people. This will come to pass when the church awakens to the truth that the saving love of God is the gift of himself, and that God himself is the gospel.

*Fear not, for behold, I bring you good news of a
great joy that will be for all the people. For unto
you is born this day in the city of David a Savior,
who is Christ the Lord.*

LUKE 2:10-11

*Now I would remind you, brothers, of the
gospel. . . . For I delivered to you as of first importance
what I also received: that Christ died for our sins
in accordance with the Scriptures, that he was buried,
that he was raised on the third day in
accordance with the Scriptures.*

1 CORINTHIANS 15:1-4

1

THE GOSPEL—
PROCLAMATION AND
EXPLANATION

I pray that one of the effects of this book will be that the gospel of Jesus Christ is heralded—proclaimed, announced, declared, broadcast—in all its magnificent fullness for all the world to hear. That is what a person does who has heard good news. He tells it. And *gospel* means good news. Good news is for proclaiming—for heralding the way an old-fashioned town crier would do.

> Hear ye! Hear ye! Hear ye! All rebels, insurgents, dissidents, and pro-testers against the King! Hear the royal decree! A great day of reck-oning is coming, a day of justice and vengeance. But now hear this, all inhabitants of the King's realm! Amnesty is herewith published by the mercy of your Sovereign. A price has been paid. All debts may be forgiven. All rebellion absolved. All dishonor pardoned. None is excluded from this offer. Lay down the weapons of rebellion, kneel in submission, receive the royal amnesty as a gift of imperial love, swear fealty to your sovereign, and rise a free and happy subject of your King.

NEWS! NEWS! NEWS!

The word for gospel in the New Testament is *euangelion* (εὐαγγέλιον). It's built out of a prefix that means good or joy-ful and a root word that means message or news. The word was used widely in the New Testament world to mean "the message of victory, but also used of political and private messages bringing joy."[1] In a period of history without print media or radio or television, the messenger with the good news delivered the news in person. It was spoken as an announcement. It had a celebrative feel to it. The messenger exulted over the news he had to bring. It was *good* news.

It is easy in our day to lose the sense of wonder and amazement at the news quality of the gospel. If we would feel what the good news of the New Testament really was, we should not forget the way it was announced in Luke 2:10-11: "The angel said to them, 'Fear not, for behold, I bring you *good news* of a great joy that will be for all the people. For unto you is born this day in the city of David a Savior, who is Christ the Lord.'"

When this news landed on the earth, the effect was extraordinary—because the news was extraordinary. Nothing like this had ever happened before. Nothing like it has ever happened since. Something absolutely new had entered history. One could even say, a whole new history began with the coming of Jesus.

WHY ARE THE PRISONERS REJOICING? NEWS!

Consider another picture of the gospel arriving. This time not the ancient town crier, but a modern prison camp. Imagine American prisoners of war held behind barbed wire in a camp with little food and filthy conditions near the end of the Second World War.[2] On the outside of the fence the captors are free and go about their business as though they don't have a care. Inside the fence the captured soldiers are thin, hollow-eyed, unshaven, and dirty. Some die each day.

Then somehow a shortwave radio is smuggled into one of the barracks. There is connection with the outside world and the progress of the war. Then one day the captors on the outside of the

---

[1] Ulrich Becker, "Gospel, Evangelize, Evangelist," in *The New International Dictionary of New Testament Theology*, 3 vols., ed. Colin Brown (Grand Rapids, Mich.: Zondervan, 1986), 2:107.
[2] I first heard this analogy from Ray Bakke told in relation to ministry in the urban centers of our country. I have adapted it for use here.

fence see something very strange. Inside the fence the weak, dirty, unshaved American soldiers are smiling and laughing, and a few who have the strength give a whoop and throw tin pans into the air.

What makes this so strange to everyone outside the fence is that nothing has changed. These American soldiers are still in captivity. They still have little food and water. And many are still sick and dying. But what the captors don't know is that what these soldiers do have is news. The enemy lines have been broken through. The decisive battle of liberation has been fought. And the liberating troops are only miles away from the camp. Freedom is imminent.

This is the difference that news makes. Christians have heard the news that Christ has come into the world and has fought the decisive battle to defeat Satan and death and sin and hell. The war will be over soon, and there is no longer any doubt as to who will win. Christ will win, and he will liberate all those who have put their hope in him.

The good news is not that there is no pain or death or sin or hell. There is. The good news is that the King himself has come, and these enemies have been defeated, and if we trust in what he has done and what he promises, we will escape the death sentence and see the glory of our Liberator and live with him forever. This news fills us with hope and joy (Rom. 15:13) and frees us from self-pity and empowers us to love those who are suffering. In this hope-sustained love he will help us persevere until the final trumpet of liberation sounds and the prison camp is made into a "new earth" (2 Pet. 3:13).

BUT WHAT DOES THE NEWS MEAN?

But the gospel is not only news. It is first news, and then it is doctrine. *Doctrine* means teaching, explaining, clarifying. Doctrine is part of the gospel because news can't be just declared by the mouth of a herald—it has to be understood in the mind of a hearer. If the town crier says, "Amnesty is herewith published by the mercy of your Sovereign," someone will ask, "What does 'amnesty' mean?" There will be many questions when the news is announced. "What is the price that has been paid?" "How have we dishonored the King?" When the gospel is proclaimed, it must be explained. What if the shortwave radio announcer used technical terminology that some of the prisoners were not sure of? Someone would need to explain it. Unintelligible good news is not even news, let alone good.

Gospel doctrine matters because the good news is so full and rich and wonderful that it must be opened like a treasure chest, and all its treasures brought out for the enjoyment of the world. Doctrine is the description of these treasures. Doctrine describes their true value and why they are so valuable. Doctrine guards the diamonds of the gospel from being discarded as mere crystals. Doctrine protects the treasures of the gospel from the pirates who don't like the diamonds but who make their living trading them for other stones. Doctrine polishes the old gems buried at the bottom of the chest. It puts the jewels of gospel truth in order on the scarlet tapestry of history so each is seen in its most beautiful place.

And all the while, doctrine does this with its head bowed in wonder that it should be allowed to touch the things of God. It whispers praise and thanks as it deals with the diamonds of the King. Its fingers tremble at the cost of what it handles. Prayers ascend for help, lest any stone be minimized or misplaced. And on its knees gospel doctrine knows it serves the herald. The gospel is not mainly about being explained. Explanation is necessary, but it is not primary. A love letter must be intelligible, but grammar and logic are not the point. Love is the point. The gospel is good news. Doctrine serves that. It serves the one whose feet are bruised (and beautiful!) from walking to the unreached places with news: "Come, listen to the news of God! Listen to what God has done! Listen! Understand! Bow! Believe!"

DEFINING THE GOOD NEWS

What then is the news? What is the message that must be proclaimed and explained? To that we turn in the next chapters. But keep in mind the angle of this book. Our question is not merely, what is the gospel? Our question is: What is the ultimate good of the gospel that makes all the aspects of good news good? What is the goal of the gospel that, if we miss it, takes all the good out of the gospel? What do we mean when we say God is the gospel?

I do not account my life of any value nor as precious to myself, if only I may finish my course and the ministry that I received from the Lord Jesus, to testify to the gospel of the grace of God.

ACTS 20:24

2

THE GOSPEL—THE BIBLICAL SCOPE OF ITS MEANING

What we will see in this chapter is how the Bible defines the gospel. But the point of the chapter in the end will be to show that many true and precious aspects of the gospel can be affirmed, and yet the final and greatest good of the gospel be missed. The manifold glories of the gospel are beautiful. But that is just the point. If the overarching beauty is not seen—namely, the beauty of the glory of Christ—then the aim of the gospel is not attained. We will come back to this point at the end of the chapter. For now let us look at the biblical facets of the gospel-diamond, and fix our eyes on the glory they intend to reveal.

HOW SHALL WE DEFINE THE GOSPEL?

How does the Bible define the gospel? Interestingly the Bible (including the Greek Old Testament[1] and New Testament) uses the noun "gospel" ($\epsilon\dot{v}\alpha\gamma\gamma\acute{\epsilon}\lambda\iota o\nu$) seventy-seven times and the verb for "preach the gospel" ($\epsilon\dot{v}\alpha\gamma\gamma\epsilon\lambda\acute{\iota}\zeta\omega$) seventy-seven times. In the vast majority of these uses the meaning is assumed rather than defined. But there are enough defining uses to give a clear picture of what the gospel is. I have structured this chapter around the uses of the word "gospel" that have definitions (or phrases that function like

---

[1] Only one of these uses ($\epsilon\dot{v}\alpha\gamma\gamma\epsilon\lambda\acute{\iota}\zeta o\mu\alpha\iota$) in the Greek Old Testament is not in the Protestant Old Testament (Psalms of Solomon 11:1).

definitions) in the immediate context. The challenge in defining such a common and broad word or phrase like "good news" or "declare good news" is to avoid two extremes. One extreme would be to define the Christian gospel so broadly that everything good in the Christian message is called gospel, and the other would be to define the Christian gospel so narrowly that the definition cannot do justice to all the uses in the New Testament. I hope to find a middle way.

THERE IS A LIVING GOD

The gospel includes the good news that there is a living God who created heaven and earth. When Paul and Barnabas came to a city of Asia Minor named Lystra, God enabled them to heal a crippled man. The crowds were stunned and cried out, "The gods have come down to us in the likeness of men!" (Acts 14:11). They called Barnabas Zeus (the king of the gods), and they called Paul Hermes (the messenger of the gods). The priest of Zeus wanted to sacrifice to them.

But at this point Paul began to preach the gospel. He started like this: "Men, why are you doing these things? We also are men, of like nature with you, and we bring you *good news [εὐαγγελιζό-μενοι], that you should turn from these vain things to a living God, who made the heaven and the earth* and the sea and all that is in them" (Acts 14:15). The "good news" includes the truth that there is a living God who created all these things.

There simply can be no good news without a living God who created the universe. No cherished aspect of the Christian gospel would have any redemptive meaning if there were no living God who created heaven and earth. So Luke, the writer of the book of Acts, says that Paul began his gospel message with the good news that there is something vastly greater than what the people of Lystra had dreamed in their religion: there is a God who lives and created all else. That is a foundational stone in the structure of the Christian gospel.

THE ARRIVAL OF GOD'S IMPERIAL AUTHORITY

The gospel not only includes the truth that God is the Creator who is alive today—it also includes the truth that he is the King of the universe who is now, in Jesus Christ, exerting his imperial authority in the world for the sake of his people. In Romans 10:15 the apostle Paul quotes Isaiah 52:7 to show that his gospel had been predicted by God. "How beautiful upon the mountains are the feet of him who brings *good news* [εὐαγγελιζομένου], who publishes peace, who brings good news [εὐαγγελιζόμενος] of happiness, who publishes salvation, who says to Zion, '*Your God reigns.*'"

Those last words define one foundational part of the good news that Isaiah foretells. "Your God reigns." God's sovereign rule is essential to the gospel. Isaiah foresaw the day when God's sovereign rule over all things would break into this world in a more open way and bring great blessing to the people of God. So when the promised Messiah came into the world, this is the primary way he spoke the gospel. "Jesus came into Galilee, proclaiming *the gospel of God*, and saying, '*The time is fulfilled, and the kingdom of God is at hand*; repent and believe in the gospel'" (Mark 1:14).[2] In other words, the reign of God has broken into this world to set things right for the sake of his people; *therefore* repent and believe this good news. In fact, if you do, you are part of his people. In a world so full of brokenness and sin, there simply can be no good news if God does not break in with kingly authority. If God does not come with sovereign rights as King of the universe, there will be only hopelessness in this world.

JESUS: A SAVIOR WHO IS CHRIST, THE LORD

As the message and ministry of Jesus Christ unfolded on earth two thousand years ago, it became clear that the arrival of the king-

---

[2] See also Luke 4:43, "He said to them, 'I must preach the good news of the kingdom of God to the other towns as well; for I was sent for this purpose.'" Luke 8:1 adds, "Soon afterward he went on through cities and villages, proclaiming and bringing the good news of the kingdom of God." Luke 16:16 says, "The Law and the Prophets were until John; since then the good news of the kingdom of God is preached, and everyone forces his way into it." For an excellent introduction to the teaching of Jesus on the kingdom of God see George Eldon Ladd, *The Presence of the Future* (Grand Rapids, Mich.: Eerdmans, 1996).

dom of God and the arrival of Jesus were the same. You can see how the gospel was summed up this way in Acts 8:12: "Philip . . . *preached good news* [εὐαγγελιζομένῳ] *about the kingdom of God and the name of Jesus Christ,* [and] they were baptized, both men and women." The reason that the coming of the kingdom of God and the coming of Jesus were the same is that Jesus was the long-awaited "son of David." He was the promised King. The gospel is the good news that the promised King of Israel had come. So Paul opens the book of Romans with this description of the gospel. It is "the *gospel* [εὐαγγέλιον] *of God, which he promised beforehand through his prophets in the holy Scriptures, concerning his Son, who was descended from David*" (1:1-3).

When the angels announced Jesus' arrival at that first Christmas, they put it all together. This was the gospel. It was the arrival of the sovereign King, the Lord. It was the arrival of the promised Messiah (which is what "Christ" means), the Son of David. And with this divine power, and with this royal lineage, the Lord Jesus Christ would become a Savior. "The angel said to them, 'Fear not, for behold, *I bring you good news* [εὐαγγελίζομαι] of a great joy that will be for all the people. For unto you is born this day in the city of David *a Savior, who is Christ the Lord*" (Luke 2:10-11). The good news is that the King of the Universe (the Lord), the Messiah (Christ), has come to be a Savior.

CHRIST DIED FOR OUR SINS IN ACCORDANCE WITH THE SCRIPTURES

How did Jesus, the Messiah, the Lord of heaven, go on to become a Savior? He tells us clearly: "For even the Son of Man came not to be served but to serve, and to give his life as a ransom for many" (Mark 10:45). He would die in order to pay a ransom so that many others would not have to perish. Similarly, at the Last Supper he said, "This cup that is poured out for you is the new covenant in my blood" (Luke 22:20). In other words, when he sheds his blood, it will be for others, and it will obtain the long-promised "new covenant" that promised, "I will forgive their iniquity, and I will remember their sin no more" (Jer. 31:34). That much Jesus made plain.

But it was the apostle Paul who made the link explicit between the word *gospel* and the death of Jesus for our sins. "Now I would remind you, brothers, of the *gospel* [εὐαγγέλιον] I preached [εὐηγγελισάμην] to you. . . . For I delivered to you as of first importance what I also received: *that Christ died for our sins in accordance with the Scriptures*" (1 Cor. 15:1-3). The coming of the King, the Lord, the Messiah, was the coming of a Savior because he died to bear our sins, not his own (since he had none, Heb. 4:15). His death was a ransom for us that we could not pay for ourselves.[3]

Jesus, Risen from the Dead as Preached in My Gospel

But there would be no gospel if Jesus had stayed dead. Paul made this crystal-clear in 1 Corinthians 15:17, "If Christ has not been raised, your faith is futile and you are still in your sins." This is why Paul's definition of the gospel in 1 Corinthians 15:1, 3-4 includes both the death and resurrection of Jesus: "I would remind you, brothers, of *the gospel* [εὐαγγέλιον] . . . that Christ died for our sins in accordance with the Scriptures, that he was buried, *that he was raised on the third day in accordance with the Scriptures*."

The King would not rule over a ransomed people if he were not raised from the dead. And if the King of kings is not ruling, there is no gospel. Jesus made clear that he would rise from the dead,[4] and Paul made clear that this was an essential part of the gospel: "Remember Jesus Christ, *risen from the dead*, the offspring

---

[3] Psalm 49:7, 8, 15 says, "Truly no man can ransom another, or give to God the price of his life, for the ransom of their life is costly and can never suffice. . . . But God will ransom my soul from the power of Sheol, for he will receive me."

[4] See Matthew 12:40, "For just as Jonah was three days and three nights in the belly of the great fish, so will the Son of Man be three days and three nights in the heart of the earth." Also Mark 8:31, "And he began to teach them that the Son of Man must suffer many things and be rejected by the elders and the chief priests and the scribes and be killed, and after three days rise again." See also Mark 9:31; 10:34. John 2:19, "Jesus answered them, 'Destroy this temple, and in three days I will raise it up.'"

of David, as preached in *my gospel* [εὐαγγέλιόν]" (2 Tim. 2:8).[5]
Therefore the living God, the Creator, the King of the universe, has
come in his Son, Jesus the Messiah, and has died for our sins and has
been raised from the dead. All this is the gospel. But there is more.

THE GOSPEL IS NOT GOOD NEWS WITHOUT
THE PROMISE OF THE SPIRIT

When John the Baptist preached the gospel, the aspect of it that he
emphasized was that the Mighty One who would be coming after
him, namely Jesus, would not baptize with water but with the Holy
Spirit and fire. He said, "I baptize you with water, but he who is
mightier than I is coming, the strap of whose sandals I am not worthy to untie. *He will baptize you with the Holy Spirit and with fire.*"
Then to show that this was part of the gospel Luke said, "So with
many other exhortations he *preached good news* [εὐηγγελίζετο] to
the people" (Luke 3:16, 18). The word "other" implies that what
he had just said was part of the good news and there are "other"
things to say as part of the gospel as well.

When Jesus was raised and went back to heaven, he did not leave
the disciples without his presence and power—his fellowship and
help. He had said to his disciples, "You know [the Spirit of truth] for
he dwells with you and will be in you. I will not leave you as orphans;
I will come to you" (John 14:17-18). In other words, when the Spirit
comes, he will be the Spirit of Christ. The Spirit will be for us the
presence and the power of Christ himself. The fellowship of Christ,
promised in the gospel, happens by the Spirit's presence in us.

In the last hours before he left, Jesus confirmed the gospel
words of John the Baptist: "Behold, I am sending the promise of my
Father upon you. But stay in the city until you are clothed with

---

[5] See also Acts 13:32-33, "We bring you the good news [εὐαγγελιζόμεθα] that what God promised to the fathers, this he has fulfilled to us their children *by raising Jesus.*" The definition Paul
gave of the gospel in Romans 1:1-4 includes the resurrection: ". . . the gospel [εὐαγγέλιον] of
God, which he promised beforehand through his prophets in the holy Scriptures, concerning
his Son, who was descended from David according to the flesh *and was declared to be the Son
of God in power according to the Spirit of holiness by his resurrection from the dead*, Jesus
Christ our Lord."

power from on high. . . . John baptized with water, but you will be baptized with the Holy Spirit not many days from now . . . you will receive power when the Holy Spirit has come upon you" (Luke 24:49; Acts 1:5, 8). The Holy Spirit is the down payment, a guarantee of the fullness of joy we will know in the perfected fellowship with the Father and the Son in the age to come (2 Cor. 1:22; 5:5). What makes the gospel good news in the end is the enjoyment of the glory of God in Christ. The Holy Spirit provides the present experience of that enjoyment. Therefore the promise of the Spirit in the gospel is what makes it good news.

THE PROMISE OF SALVATION FOR ALL WHO BELIEVE

On the basis of all that news—news of things God has already done in Christ without yet any effect in us—now the Bible speaks of the *effects* or the *accomplishments* of those events as good news. One of the most encompassing words to describe the good news of what God does *for* us and *in* us is *salvation*. Paul refers to "the gospel of your salvation" in Ephesians 1:13. "In him you also, when you heard the word of truth, *the gospel* [εὐαγγέλιον] *of your salvation,* and believed in him, were sealed with the promised Holy Spirit."

Paul says in Romans 1:16, "I am not ashamed of *the gospel* [εὐαγγέλιον], for it is the power of God *for salvation* to everyone who believes, to the Jew first and also to the Greek." How then should we speak of salvation in relation to the gospel? Should we speak of salvation only as the result of the gospel or as part of the gospel? The text says that the gospel is the power of God *for* salvation. Some might therefore conclude that salvation is not part of the gospel.

The trouble here is that we need to distinguish the *experience* of salvation in particular persons and the *promise* of salvation through believing in Christ. The actual experience of a particular person's being saved is not part of the gospel. But that experience happens when the person believes the gospel, and part of what they believe is the promise that on the basis of the death and resurrection of Jesus they *will* be saved. So the way we should say it is that the *promise* of salvation *is* part of the gospel, but the actual *experience* of salvation in particular persons is not part of the gospel, but the result of the gospel. What Romans 1:16 makes plain is that "to everyone who believes," the promise of salvation becomes personally true for them. So, yes, the gospel is the good news that, because of the death and resurrection of Jesus, salvation comes to believers. Therefore, it is the power of God for salvation to everyone who believes.

This all-encompassing word, *salvation,* embraces all the gospel promises, such as the promise of healing, help for the poor, liberty for captives, peace, eternal life, global expanse, and the all-satisfying vision of the glory of God.

What the Cross Purchased Makes the Cross Good News

When Jesus healed the sick and cast out demons and raised the dead and helped the poor, he was demonstrating what made "the gospel of the kingdom" good news. "He went throughout all Galilee, teaching in their synagogues and *proclaiming the gospel* [εὐαγγέλιον] *of the kingdom and healing every disease* and every affliction among the people" (Matt. 4:23). As he opened his ministry in Nazareth, Jesus said, "The Spirit of the Lord is upon me, because he has anointed me *to proclaim good news* [εὐαγγελίσασθαι] *to the poor. He has sent me to proclaim liberty to the captives and recovering of sight to the blind, to set at liberty those who are oppressed*" (Luke 4:18). These were the kinds of blessings that mark the reign of God in this age partly, and in the age to come completely.

What the progress of revelation shows, as the New Testament unfolds, is that the death and resurrection of Christ to cover our sins is the foundation for all these blessings that the gospel of the kingdom announces. The King must die before he reigns. Otherwise the justice of his reign would only bring judgment and not salvation. So all the kingdom blessings demonstrated in the Gospels had to be purchased by the blood of Christ. This is why the cross must ever be the center and foundation of the gospel and why the blessings of the gospel should only be called gospel in relation to the cross.

THE GOOD NEWS OF PEACE WITH GOD AND EACH OTHER

Alongside healing and help for the poor and liberty for the captives proclaimed by Jesus as good news, Paul and Peter speak of peace with God and eternal life and global expanse as part of what the good news is. For example, Peter described the gospel that God sent through Jesus as "the word that [God] sent to Israel, *preaching good news* [εὐαγγελιζόμενος] *of peace* through Jesus Christ" (Acts 10:36). And Paul spoke of having our feet shod with "the readiness given by *the gospel* [εὐαγγελίου] *of peace*" (Eph. 6:15). This peace that the gospel promises and creates is first between man and God (Rom. 5:10; 2 Cor. 5:18), and secondly between people. When different ethnic groups share a common vertical reconciliation, it produces a horizontal one (Eph. 2:14-18).

THE GOOD NEWS PROMISES ETERNAL LIFE

The effect of this peace with God is eternal life. This too is what makes the gospel of Christ good news. Paul says in 2 Timothy 1:10: "[God's grace] has been manifested through the appearing of our Savior Christ Jesus, who abolished death and *brought life and immortality to light through the gospel* [εὐαγγελίου]." The gospel makes clear what God has achieved in the death and resurrection of Jesus, literally, "life and incorruptibility." William Mounce says that "'incorruptibility' [ἀφθαρσίαν], when joined with ζωή, 'life,' is synonymous with eternal life."[6] I think that's right. The reason the gospel brings eternal life to light is that it makes crystal-clear *why* eternal life is possible (the death and resurrection of Jesus) and *what* eternal life will be (life with the risen Christ).

"IN YOU SHALL ALL THE NATIONS BE BLESSED"

The good news of all that Christ achieved when he died and rose again embraces all the peoples of the earth. This is not just a com-

---

[6] William Mounce, *Pastoral Epistles, Word Biblical Commentary*, vol. 46 (Nashville: Thomas Nelson, 2000), 485.

ment about how far the good news reaches. This is part of what makes the good news good. The gospel of the kingdom would not be good news if the King did not rule among all the peoples. Paul explicitly identifies the blessing of the nations as part of the gospel. For example, in Galatians 3:8 he says, "The Scripture, foreseeing that God would justify the Gentiles by faith, *preached the gospel beforehand* [προευηγγελίσατο] to Abraham, saying, '*In you shall all the nations be blessed.*'" Preaching the gospel means announcing the good news that all the nations will be blessed through Abraham—that is, through the death and resurrection of Abraham's seed, Jesus Christ (Gal. 3:16).

The gospel message includes the truth "that *the Gentiles are fellow heirs*, members of the same body, and partakers of the promise in Christ Jesus *through the gospel* [εὐαγγελίου]" (Eph. 3:6). The fact that the salvation of the nations happens "through the gospel" does not mean that the gospel is defined without the promise of that salvation. It means that the promise of global Gentile salvation, based on the death and resurrection of Jesus, is the means of bringing that salvation about. The *actual* salvation of the nations comes through the blood-bought *promise* of Gentile salvation in the gospel. If the gospel were parochial, it would not be the gospel.

"The Gospel of the Grace of God"

The gospel contains the news of its ground. The ground of all the good news is God's grace. This is why Paul calls his message "the gospel of the grace of God." One of his most moving testimonies is found with these very words in Acts 20:24, "I do not account my life of any value nor as precious to myself, if only I may finish my course and the ministry that I received from the Lord Jesus, to testify to the *gospel* [εὐαγγέλιον] *of the grace of God.*" More than once the gospel is called " the word of his grace" (Acts 14:3; 20:32). The gospel is the good news of what God's grace promises to sinners and how he achieves it through Christ.

Grace is the free blessing of God that flows from his heart to guilty, undeserving sinners. Therefore in relation to our salvation it is the opposite of human initiative or merit. This is what Paul means with his fundamental statement, "It is no longer on the basis of works; otherwise grace would no longer be grace" (Rom. 11:6). In this statement he was referring to our being chosen by God: "There is a remnant, *chosen* by grace" (Rom. 11:5), or literally, "a remnant according to the *election* of grace." Before we had done anything good or evil, God chose us in Christ. The freedom of grace is stressed because its origin is in eternity where we were chosen: "He chose us in him *before the foundation of the world* . . . to the praise of his glorious *grace*" (Eph. 1:4, 6). God's grace is the ground of all gospel blessings.

JESUS' DEATH MAKES GOD'S GOSPEL GRACE JUST

The decisive act of God's grace was the central gospel event of Christ's coming and suffering: "You know *the grace of our Lord Jesus Christ*, that though he was rich, yet for your sake he became poor, so that you by his poverty might become rich" (2 Cor. 8:9). Jesus suffered and died "so that *by the grace of God* he might taste death for everyone" (Heb. 2:9). The death of Jesus in our place was the act of God's grace that makes all acts of grace righteous in God's sight. It is not obvious that acquitting the guilty is a righteous thing for a judge to do ("He who justifies the wicked and he who condemns the righteous are both alike an abomination to the LORD," Prov. 17:15). Therefore since God is just as well as gracious, he sent Christ to bear the just punishment for sin, so that he might "show God's righteousness" (Rom. 3:25). "It was to show his righteousness at the present time, so that he might be just and the justifier of the one who has faith in Jesus" (Rom. 3:26). Therefore God is just in being gracious in the gospel.

THE GRACE OF THE GOSPEL IS THE GROUND OF EVERY GOOD PROMISE

From this central act of gospel grace flows a mighty river of gracious gospel blessings. The calling of God that wakened us from our sin-soaked sleep of death was owing to grace. God "*called* us to a holy calling, not because of our works but because of his own purpose and *grace*" (2 Tim. 1:9). We responded in faith not because our wills were by nature compliant. Rather we believed because God's grace enabled us to believe. "*By grace* you have been saved through faith. And this is not your own doing; it is the gift of God" (Eph. 2:8). "The *grace* of our Lord overflowed for me with the faith and love that are in Christ Jesus" (1 Tim. 1:14). When Apollos worked in Achaia, Luke says, "he greatly helped those who *through grace* had believed" (Acts 18:27). That any of us has believed is owing to the mighty work of God's grace—the grace made possible by the blood of Christ. And this blood-bought grace is essential to what makes the good news good.

In the presence of this gracious gift of faith, God *justifies* us "by his grace" (Rom. 3:24; Tit. 3:7) and *forgives* our trespasses "according to the riches of his grace" (Eph. 1:7) and *saves* us "through the grace of the Lord Jesus" (Acts 15:11) and "makes all grace abound" to us for "*every good work*" (2 Cor. 9:8) and makes his grace sufficient for all our *affliction* (2 Cor. 12:9) and enables us "by the grace of God" to *work harder* than we imagined we could (1 Cor. 15:10) and grants "grace to *help* in time of need" (Heb. 4:16) and gives us "eternal *comfort* and good *hope* through grace" (2 Thess. 2:16), so that in the end "the name of our Lord *Jesus may be glorified* in you, and *you in him*, according to the grace of our God and the Lord Jesus Christ" (2 Thess. 1:12).

In other words, every blessing that comes to redeemed sinners comes on the ground and by the power of God's grace. By grace God sent the Son to die, and by that death everything we need in order to be eternally happy in God is ours. "He who did not spare his own Son but gave him up for us all, how will he not also with him graciously give us all things?" (Rom. 8:32). The gospel is the good news that because God did not spare Christ, he will not spare any omnipotent effort to give us everything that is good for us.

No Good Thing in the Gospel Is Good Without the Final Supreme Good: God

Now the point of this book must be pressed. The point is that the precious gospel events and gospel blessings that I have outlined in this chapter do not suffice to make the gospel good news. What makes the gospel finally and supremely good news has not yet been mentioned. We saw a glimpse of it in the section on the Holy Spirit when I said:

> When the Spirit comes, he will be the Spirit of Christ. The Spirit will be for us the presence and the power of Christ himself. The fellowship of Christ, promised in the gospel, happens by the Spirit's presence in us. . . . What makes the gospel good news in the end is the enjoyment of the glory of God in Christ. The Holy Spirit provides the present experience of that enjoyment. Therefore the promise of the Spirit in the gospel is what makes it good news.

Another brief glimpse happened when I observed that the gospel gives us "good *hope* through grace" (2 Thess. 2:16), so that in the end "the name of our Lord Jesus may be glorified in you, and you in him, according to the grace of our God and the Lord Jesus Christ" (2 Thess. 1:12).

But for the most part the good things mentioned in this chapter as essential parts of the gospel are not the final good of the gospel and would not prove to be good for us at all if the unmentioned supreme good were not seen and embraced. That good is God himself seen and savored in all his glory. Focusing on facets of a diamond without seeing the beauty of the whole is demeaning to the diamond. If the hearers of the gospel do not see the glory of Christ, the image of God, in all the events and gifts of the gospel, they do not see what finally makes the gospel good news. If you embrace everything that I have mentioned in this chapter about the facets of the gospel, but do it in a way that does not make the glory of God in Christ your supreme treasure, then you have not embraced the gospel.

Until the gospel *events* of Good Friday and Easter and the gospel *promises* of justification and eternal life lead you to behold and embrace *God himself* as your highest joy, you have not embraced the gospel of God. You have embraced some of his gifts. You have rejoiced over some of his rewards. You have marveled at some of his miracles. But you have not yet been awakened to why the gifts, the rewards, and the miracles have come. They have come for one great reason: that you might behold forever the glory of God in Christ, and by beholding become the kind of person who delights in God above all things, and by delighting display his supreme beauty and worth with ever-increasing brightness and bliss forever.

Which leads us now in the next chapter to talk about the ultimate goal of the gospel—the ultimate *good* that the *good* news offers. I have named it, but now I must show it from the Scriptures.

Get you up to a high mountain, O Zion, herald of
good news; lift up your voice with strength,
O Jerusalem, herald of good news; lift it up, fear not;
say to the cities of Judah, "Behold your God!"

ISAIAH 40:9

3

THE GOSPEL—"BEHOLD YOUR GOD!"

In the last chapter we unfolded the broader biblical meaning of the Christian gospel. It included the existence of the living God and his coming into history with imperial authority over all things as the long-awaited King of Israel and Lord of the universe. This King was Jesus Christ, the Messiah, the Savior. He fulfilled the Old Testament expectations of the Son of David, died for our sins, was buried, and rose again triumphant over Satan, death, and hell. He promised his own Spirit to be with us and help us. On the basis of his death and resurrection, the gospel promises a great salvation— eventual healing from disease and liberation from oppression, peace with God and others who believe, justification by faith apart from works of the law, forgiveness of sins, transformation into the image of Christ, eternal life, and the global inclusion of all people from all nations in this salvation.

CHRIST SUFFERED TO BRING US TO GOD

But the point was made that the final and greatest good of the gospel is not included in that array of gospel gifts. My burden in this book is to make as clear as I can that preachers can preach on these great aspects of the gospel and yet never take people to the goal of the gospel. Preachers can say dozens of true and wonderful things about the gospel and not lead people to where the gospel is leading.

People can hear the gospel preached, or read it in their Bibles, and not see the final aim of the gospel that makes the good news good.

What makes all the events of Good Friday and Easter and all the promises they secure good news is that they lead us to God. "Christ also suffered once for sins, the righteous for the unrighteous, *that he might bring us to God*" (1 Pet. 3:18). And when we get there, it is God himself who will satisfy our souls forever. Everything else in the gospel is meant to display God's glory and remove every obstacle in him (such as his wrath) and in us (such as our rebellion) so that we can enjoy him forever. God is the gospel. That is, he is what makes the good news good. Nothing less can make the gospel good news. God is the final and highest gift that makes the good news good. Until people use the gospel to get to God, they use it wrongly.

JUSTIFICATION DEALS WITH OUR GREATEST PROBLEM

Before we spread out the biblical support for this claim, let me try to show how even some of the brightest facets of the gospel-diamond can so fixate our attention that we do not see the glory of God reflected in the entire diamond itself.

Take justification, for example. Few facets of the gospel are more precious to me than this. I wrote a whole book to show why this doctrine is the heart of the gospel and why it includes the imputation of Christ's righteousness to us by faith alone apart from works of the law.[1] I won't go into that defense here except to quote some proven voices. For example, G. C. Berkouwer wrote, "The confession of divine justification touches man's life at its heart, at the point of its relationship to God. It defines the preaching of the Church, the existence and progress of the life of faith, the root of human security and man's perspective for the future."[2]

The most fundamental need of man that the gospel addresses is addressed by the gift of justification. We are not merely alienated

---

[1] John Piper, *Counted Righteous in Christ: Should We Abandon the Imputation of Christ's Righteousness?* (Wheaton, Ill.: Crossway Books, 2002).
[2] G. C. Berkouwer, *Faith and Justification* (Grand Rapids, Mich.: Eerdmans, 1954), 17.

from God but are under his wrath (John 3:36; Rom. 1:18; 5:9; Gal. 3:10). This means that what must change fundamentally is God's anger toward us because of our God-dishonoring sin (Rom. 3:23). We are not capable of changing God. We cannot pay our own debt. "Truly no man can ransom another, or give to God the price of his life" (Ps. 49:7). Therefore, in his great mercy, God intervened to put Christ forward as the propitiation of God's own wrath (Rom. 3:25). Christ absorbed the curse that we deserved (Gal. 3:13). "He himself bore our sins in his body on the tree" (1 Pet. 2:24).

THE GREAT EXCHANGE

But not only are our sins counted as his, his righteousness is counted as ours. This has been called "the great exchange." For example, J. I. Packer writes, "The judge declares guilty sinners immune from punishment and righteous in his sight. The *great exchange* is no legal fiction, no arbitrary pretence, no mere word-game on God's part, but a costly achievement."[3] The biblical statement of "the great exchange" is 2 Corinthians 5:21, "For our sake he made him to be sin who knew no sin, so that in him we might become the righteousness of God."

Thus justification has these two sides: the removal of sin because Christ bears our curse, and the imputation of righteousness because we are in Christ and his righteousness is counted as ours.[4] Thus Calvin defines justification as "the acceptance with which God receives us into his favor as righteous men. And we say that it consists in the remission of sins and the imputation of Christ's righteousness."[5] Similarly Luther (who called the doctrine of justification the belief that determines whether the church stands or falls[6]) affirmed both these aspects of justification: "Christ took all

---

[3] J. I. Packer, "Justification in Protestant Theology," in *Honoring the People of God, the Collected Shorter Writings of J. I. Packer,* 4 vols. (Carlisle, Cumbria, UK: Paternoster, 1999), 4:227. Emphasis added.

[4] To defend this statement was the burden of the book cited above: John Piper, *Counted Righteous in Christ.*

[5] John Calvin, *Institutes of the Christian Religion,* 2 vols., ed. John T. McNeill, trans. Ford Lewis Battles (Philadelphia: Westminster Press, 1960), 1:727 (III.11.2).

[6] Cited in Packer, "Justification in Protestant Theology," 19.

our sins upon him, and for them died upon the cross," and "they are righteous because they believe in Christ, whose righteousness covers them and is imputed to them."[7]

JUSTIFICATION IS THE HEART OF THE GOSPEL, NOT ITS HIGHEST GOOD

Therefore, Protestants have viewed the doctrine of justification (by grace alone, through faith alone, on the basis of Christ's blood and righteousness alone, for the glory of God alone, as taught with final authority in Scripture alone) as "the heart of the biblical Gospel."[8] I agree with that judgment. I am thrilled to call justification the heart of the gospel. But figurative language (like "heart" and "center") is ambiguous. What does it mean? By "heart" I mean that justification addresses the main problem between God and man most directly (see above) and becomes, therefore, the sustaining source of all the other benefits of the gospel.

That gives a special edge to the key question of this book: Why is justification good news? What is good about being justified by faith alone? Or more broadly, why is the gospel, which has justification by faith at its heart, good news? Now this question is seldom asked, because being forgiven for our sins and being acquitted in court for capital crimes and being counted righteous before a holy God is so manifestly a happy situation that it seems impertinent to ask, why is it good news?

But I believe we must emphatically ask this question. For the answer to it is infinitely important. Every person should be required to answer the question, "Why is it good news to you that your sins are forgiven?" "Why is it good news to you that you stand righteous in the courtroom of the Judge of the universe?" The reason this must be asked is that there are seemingly biblical answers that totally ignore the gift of God himself. A person may answer,

---

[7] Quoted in ibid., 225-226.

[8] "The heart of the biblical Gospel was to [the Reformers] God's free gift of righteousness and justification. Here was the sum and substance of that *sola fide—sola gratia—solo Christo—sola Scriptura—soli Deo gloria*, which was the sustained theme of their proclamation, polemics, praises and prayers." Ibid., 219.

"Being forgiven is good news because I don't want to go to hell." Or a person may answer, "Being forgiven is good news because a guilty conscience is a horrible thing, and I get great relief when I believe my sins are forgiven." Or a person may answer, "I want to go to heaven." But then we must ask *why* they want to go to heaven. They might answer, "Because the alternative is painful." Or "because my deceased wife is there." Or "because there will be a new heaven and a new earth where justice and beauty will finally be everywhere."

What's wrong with these answers? It's true that no one should want to go to hell. Forgiveness does indeed relieve a guilty conscience. In heaven we will be restored to loved ones who died in Christ, and we will escape the pain of hell and enjoy the justice and the beauty of the new earth. All that is true. So what's wrong with those answers? What's wrong with them is that they do not treat God as the final and highest good of the gospel. They do not express a supreme desire to be with God. God was not even mentioned. Only his gifts were mentioned. These gifts are precious. But they are not God. And they are not the gospel if God himself is not cherished as the supreme gift of the gospel. That is, if God is not treasured as the ultimate gift of the gospel, none of his gifts will be gospel, good news. And if God is treasured as the supremely valuable gift of the gospel, then all the other lesser gifts will be enjoyed as well.

Justification is not an end in itself. Neither is the forgiveness of sins or the imputation of righteousness. Neither is escape from hell or entrance into heaven or freedom from disease or liberation from bondage or eternal life or justice or mercy or the beauties of a pain-free world. None of these facets of the gospel-diamond is the chief good or highest goal of the gospel. Only one thing is: seeing and savoring God himself, being changed into the image of his Son so that more and more we delight in and display God's infinite beauty and worth.[9]

---

[9] See Chapter 11 for the explanation of the relationship between the goal of seeing God and the goal of being like God.

WHY DO I WANT TO BE FORGIVEN?

Consider an illustration of what I am trying to say. Suppose I get up in the morning and as I am walking to the bathroom I trip over some of my wife's laundry that she left lying on the hall floor. Instead of simply moving the laundry myself and assuming the best in her, I react in a way that is all out of proportion to the situation and say something very harsh to my wife just as she is waking up. She gets up, puts the laundry away, and walks downstairs ahead of me. I can tell by the silence and from my own conscience that our relationship is in serious trouble.

As I go downstairs my conscience is condemning me. Yes, the laundry should not have been there. Yes, I might have broken my neck. But those thoughts are mainly the self-defending flesh talking. The truth is that my words were way out of line. Not only was the emotional harshness out of proportion to the seriousness of the fault, but the Bible tells me to overlook the fault. "Why not rather suffer wrong? Why not rather be defrauded?" (1 Cor. 6:7).

So as I enter the kitchen there is ice in the air, and her back is blatantly toward me as she works at the kitchen counter. What needs to happen here? The answer is plain: I need to apologize and ask for forgiveness. That would be the right thing to do. But here's the analogy: Why do I want her forgiveness? So that she will make my favorite breakfast? So that my guilt feelings will go away and I will be able to concentrate at work today? So there will be good sex tonight? So the kids won't see us at odds? So that she will finally admit the laundry shouldn't have been there?

It may be that every one of those desires would come true. But they are all defective motives for wanting her forgiveness. What's missing is this: I want to be forgiven so that I will have the sweet fellowship of my wife back. She is the reason I want to be forgiven. I want the relationship restored. Forgiveness is simply a way of getting obstacles out of the way so that we can look at each other again with joy.

WOULD YOU BE HAPPY IN HEAVEN IF GOD WERE NOT THERE?

My point in this book is that all the saving events and all the saving blessings of the gospel are means of getting obstacles out of the way so that we might know and enjoy God most fully. Propitiation, redemption, forgiveness, imputation, sanctification, liberation, healing, heaven—none of these is good news except for one reason: they bring us to God for our everlasting enjoyment of him. If we believe all these things have happened to us, but do not embrace them for the sake of getting to God, they have not happened to us. Christ did not die to forgive sinners who go on treasuring anything above seeing and savoring God. And people who would be happy in heaven if Christ were not there, will not be there. The gospel is not a way to get people to heaven; it is a way to get people to God. It's a way of overcoming every obstacle to everlasting joy in God. If we don't want God above all things, we have not been converted by the gospel.

WHAT IS THE SUPREME GOOD THAT MAKES THE GOSPEL GOOD NEWS?

So now we must turn to the biblical basis for this truth. We have seen the broad biblical definition of the gospel, and have focused on the heart of the gospel in justification. Now we must inquire: What is the ultimate good of the gospel? What is its goal? What supreme good makes all the other aspects of the gospel good?

For this we turn first to a great Old Testament declaration of the gospel found in Isaiah 40:9: "Get you up to a high mountain, O Zion, herald of good news [ὁ εὐαγγελιζόμενος, LXX]; lift up your voice with strength, O Jerusalem, herald of good news [ὁ εὐαγγελιζόμενος, LXX]; lift it up, fear not; say to the cities of Judah, '*Behold your God!*'"

THE GREAT GOSPEL LONGING: SHOW ME YOUR GLORY

The ultimate good made possible by the death and resurrection of Christ, and offered in the gospel, is: "Behold your God!" Moses had pleaded for this gift as he wrestled for God's presence for the journey to the Promised Land: "Moses said, 'Please *show me your glory*'" (Ex. 33:18). King David expressed the uniqueness of this blessing in Psalm 27: "One thing have I asked of the LORD, that will I seek after: that I may dwell in the house of the LORD all the days of my life, *to gaze upon the beauty of the LORD* and to inquire in his temple. . . . You have said, 'Seek my face.' My heart says to you, '*Your face, LORD*, do I seek'" (vv. 4, 8). The memory of these encounters with God sustains David in his afflictions: "O God, you are my God; earnestly I seek you; my soul thirsts for you; my flesh faints for you, as in a dry and weary land where there is no water. So *I have looked upon you in the sanctuary, beholding your power and glory*" (Ps. 63:1-2).

We know that seeing God is in two senses impossible: *morally* we are not good enough in our fallen condition and would be consumed in the fire of his holiness if we saw him fully for who he is. This is why God showed Moses his "back" and not his face: "You cannot see my face, for man shall not see me and live" (Ex. 33:20). So God put Moses in a rock, passed by, and said, "You shall see my back, but my face shall not be seen" (v. 23).

But the impossibility of seeing God is not just because of our moral condition. It is also because he is God and we are not. This seems to be the meaning of 1 Timothy 6:16: "[He] alone has immortality, who dwells in unapproachable light, whom no one has ever seen or can see. To him be honor and eternal dominion. Amen." Created beings simply cannot look on the Creator and see him for who he is.[10]

Therefore the gazing on God in the Old Testament was mediated. There was something in between. God revealed himself in

---

[10] I take the passages of Scripture that seem like exceptions to this (like Genesis 32:30, "Jacob called the name of the place Peniel, saying, 'For I have seen God face to face, and yet my life has been delivered'") as statements along the lines of Psalm 27:4, 8 where seeing God's face means seeing reflections and evidences of his brightness and favor. Some of these reflections of God are so remarkable that witnesses speak of seeing God himself—but we need not think they mean with no mediator at all. John Sailhamer comments on Genesis 32:30, "Jacob's remark did not necessarily mean that the 'man' with whom Jacob wrestled was in fact God. Rather, as with other similar statements (e.g., Judg 13:22), when one saw the 'angel of the LORD,' it was appropriate to say that he had seen the face of God." *Genesis*, in *The Expositor's Bible Commentary*, 12 vols., ed. Frank E. Gaebelein (Grand Rapids, Mich.: Zondervan, 1990), 1:210.

deeds (Ps. 77:11-13) and visionary forms (e.g., Ezek. 1:28) and nature (Ps. 19:1) and angels (Judges 13:21-22) and especially by his word: "The LORD *appeared* again at Shiloh, for the LORD *revealed himself* to Samuel at Shiloh *by the word of the LORD*" (1 Sam. 3:21).

THE GLORY OF THE LORD SHALL BE REVEALED— IN JESUS CHRIST

But the day would come when the glory of the Lord would be revealed and seen in a new way. This was the greatest hope and expectation in the Old Testament. "A voice cries: 'In the wilderness prepare the way of the LORD; make straight in the desert a highway for our God. Every valley shall be lifted up, and every mountain and hill be made low; the uneven ground shall become level, and the rough places a plain. And *the glory of the LORD* shall be revealed, and all flesh shall see it together, for the mouth of the LORD has spoken'" (Isa. 40:3-5). "Arise, shine, for your light has come, and *the glory of the LORD* has risen upon you. For behold, darkness shall cover the earth, and thick darkness the peoples; but the LORD will arise upon you, and *his glory will be seen upon you*. And nations shall come to your light, and kings to the brightness of your rising" (Isa. 60:1-3). "The time is coming to gather all nations and tongues. And they shall come and shall *see my glory*" (Isa. 66:18).

This day dawned with the coming of Jesus. He was the Word of God and was truly God and was the incarnate manifestation of the glory of God. "In the beginning was the Word, and the Word was with God, and the Word was God. . . . And the Word became flesh and dwelt among us, and *we have seen his glory*, glory as of the only Son from the Father, full of grace and truth" (John 1:1, 14). When he worked his wonders, the glory that people saw, if they believed, was the glory of God. Jesus said to Martha, just before he raised her brother Lazarus from the dead, "Did I not tell you that if you believed you would *see the glory of God*?" (John 11:40).

MORE OF GOD APPEARED THAN THE
PROPHETS DREAMED

The glory of the Lord has risen upon the world more fully and wonderfully than the prophets imagined. They knew that the Messiah would come and that he would manifest the righteousness and faithfulness of God as never before. But they could not see plainly,[11] as we can see, that in Jesus "the whole fullness of deity dwells bodily" (Col. 2:9), that he is in the Father and the Father is in him, and the two are one (John 10:30, 38). They would have been stunned speechless to hear Jesus say to Philip, "Have I been with you so long, and you still do not know me, Philip? Whoever has seen me has seen the Father. How can you say, 'Show us the Father'?" (John 14:9). Or to hear Jesus say the simple and breathtaking words, "Before Abraham was, I am" (John 8:58).

This is why the apostle Paul called Jesus "the Christ who is *God over all*, blessed forever" (Rom. 9:5), and why he described Christ in his incarnation as being "*in the form of God*" (Phil. 2:6).[12] But Jesus did not "count *equality with God* a thing to be grasped." That is, he did not demand that he hold on to all its manifestations and avoid the humiliation of the incarnation. Rather he was willing to lay down the outward manifestations of deity and take the form of a servant and be born in the likeness of men (Phil. 2:6-7). This is why Paul described Jesus' second coming as "the appearing of the glory of *our great God* and Savior Jesus Christ" (Tit. 2:13).

---

[11] First Peter 1:10-11 says, "Concerning this salvation, the prophets who prophesied about the grace that was to be yours searched and inquired carefully, inquiring what person or time the Spirit of Christ in them was indicating when he predicted the sufferings of Christ and the subsequent glories."

[12] Being in the "form of God" (ἐν μορφῇ θεοῦ) does *not* mean that he is *only* in the "form" of God and therefore not really God. "Form" (μορφῇ) gets its meaning from the following phrase, "equality with God" (ἴσα θεῷ) and from the human counterpart language in Philippians 2:7, "taking the *form* of a servant, being born in the *likeness* of men" (μορφὴν δούλου λαβών, ἐν ὁμοιώματι ἀνθρώπων). The parallel language is to show that Christ was really man and was really God. See one of the most exhaustive studies of this crucial text, Ralph P. Martin, *CARMEN CHRISTI: Philippians 2:5-11 in Recent Interpretation and in the Setting of Early Christian Worship* (Cambridge, Mass.: Cambridge University Press, 1967).

This is why we find in the book of Hebrews these stunning words about Jesus, "But of the Son [God] says, 'Your throne, O God, is forever and ever.' . . . And, 'You, Lord, laid the foundation of the earth in the beginning, and the heavens are the work of your hands" (1:8, 10). We may conclude from these and other words about Jesus that the time finally arrived for the revelation of God in a way no one had fully dreamed: God himself, the divine Son, would become man. And human beings would see the glory of God in a way they had never seen it before. Formerly, the Bible says, God spoke by prophets, but in these last days—the days since Jesus came—God "has spoken to us by his Son, whom he appointed the heir of all things, through whom also he created the world. *He is the radiance of the glory of God and the exact imprint of his nature,* and he upholds the universe by the word of his power" (Heb. 1:2-3). When we see Jesus, we see the glory of God as in no other manifestation.[13]

THE EXCELLENCY OF CHRIST THAT NOT EVERYONE SAW

Of course, there were many who saw Jesus and did not see the glory of God. They saw a glutton and a drunkard (Matt. 11:19). They saw Beelzebul, the prince of demons (Matt. 10:25; 12:24). They saw an impostor (Matt. 27:63). "Seeing they do not see, and hearing they do not hear" (Matt. 13:13). The glory of God in the life and ministry of Jesus was not the blinding glory that we will see when he comes the second time with "his face . . . like the sun shining in full strength" (Rev. 1:16; cf. Luke 9:29). His glory, in his first coming, was the incomparably exquisite array of spiritual, moral, intellectual, verbal, and practical perfections that manifest themselves in a kind of meek miracle-working and

---

[13] When the Bible says that "The heavens declare the glory of God" (Ps. 19:1), it means something fundamentally different from when it says that Christ is the radiance of God's glory. Nowhere does the Bible say or hint that nature is God. But frequently the Bible says and shows that Jesus is God.

unanswerable teaching and humble action that set Jesus apart from all men.[14]

What I am trying to express here is that the glory of Christ, as he appeared among us, consisted not in one attribute or another, and not in one act or another, but in what Jonathan Edwards called "an admirable conjunction of diverse excellencies."[15] In a sermon titled "The Excellency of Christ" Edwards took as his text Revelation 5:5-6 where Christ is compared both to a lion and a lamb. His point was that the unique glory of Christ was that such diverse excellencies (lion and lamb) unite in him. These excellencies are so diverse that they "would have seemed to us utterly incompatible in the same subject."[16] In other words,

- we admire him for his glory, but even more because his glory is mingled with humility;
- we admire him for his transcendence, but even more because his transcendence is accompanied by condescension;
- we admire him for his uncompromising justice, but even more because it is tempered with mercy;
- we admire him for his majesty, but even more because it is a majesty in meekness;
- we admire him because of his equality with God, but even more because as God's equal he nevertheless has a deep reverence for God;

---

[14] Commenting on Peter's assurance of faith after seeing the outward glory of Christ on the mount of transfiguration (Matt. 17:1-9), where, Peter said, "we were eyewitnesses of his majesty" (2 Pet. 1:16), Jonathan Edwards explains the difference between this "outward glory" and the "spiritual glory" that one sees with the eyes of the heart: "If a sight of Christ's outward glory might give a rational assurance of his divinity, why may not an apprehension of his spiritual glory do so too? Doubtless Christ's spiritual glory is in itself as distinguishing, and as plainly showing his divinity, as his outward glory; and a great deal more: for his spiritual glory is that wherein his divinity consists; and the outward glory of his transfiguration showed him to be divine, only as it was a remarkable image or representation of that spiritual glory. Doubtless therefore he that has had a clear sight of the spiritual glory of Christ, may say, 'I have not followed cunningly devised fables, but have been an eyewitness of his majesty,' upon as good grounds as the Apostle, when he had respect to the outward glory of Christ, that he had seen." "A Divine and Supernatural Light," in *Sermons and Discourses 1730-1733*, in *The Works of Jonathan Edwards*, vol. 17, ed. Mark Valeri (New Haven, Conn.: Yale University Press, 1999), 419.

[15] Jonathan Edwards, "The Excellency of Christ," in *Sermons And Discourses 1734-1738*, in *The Works of Jonathan Edwards*, vol. 19, ed. M. X. Lesser (New Haven, Conn.: Yale University Press, 2001), 565.

[16] Ibid.

- we admire him because of how worthy he was of all good, but even more because this was accompanied by an amazing patience to suffer evil;
- we admire him because of his sovereign dominion over the world, but even more because this dominion was clothed with a spirit of obedience and submission;
- we love the way he stumped the proud scribes with his wisdom, and we love it even more because he could be simple enough to like children and spend time with them;
- and we admire him because he could still the storm, but even more because he refused to use that power to strike the Samaritans with lightning (Luke 9:54-55) and he refused to use it to get himself down from the cross.

The list could go on and on. But this is enough to illustrate that beauty and excellency in Christ is not a simple thing. It is complex. It is a coming together in one person of the perfect balance and proportion of extremely diverse qualities. And that's what makes Jesus Christ uniquely glorious, excellent, and admirable. The human heart was made to stand in awe of such ultimate excellence. We were made to admire Jesus Christ, the Son of God.

Seeing They Did Not See, Because They Loved the Glory of Men

But not everyone saw. Having eyes some did not see. But those who had eyes to see saw the glory of God when Christ was on the earth. Jesus said that only those who believe can see this glory. For example, when Martha worried that her dead brother would not be raised by Jesus, he said, "Did I not tell you that *if you believed* you would see the glory of God?" (John 11:40). Some saw Lazarus raised from the dead, but did not see the glory of God.[17] "Many of

---

[17] "The real meaning of what He would do is accessible only to faith. All there, believing or not, would see the miracle. But Jesus is promising Martha a sight of the glory." Leon Morris, *The Gospel According to John* (Grand Rapids, Mich.: Eerdmans, 1971), 560. "What he intended to convey was this, that if Martha would only stop thinking about that corpse and would rivet her

the Jews therefore, who had come with Mary and had seen what [Jesus] did, believed in him, *but some of them went to the Pharisees and told them what Jesus had done*" (John 11:45-46).[18]

The glory of Christ is not synonymous with raw power. The glory is the divine beauty of his manifold perfections. To see this requires a change of heart. Jesus makes that clear when he asks, "How can you believe, when you receive glory from one another and do not seek the glory that comes from the only God?" (John 5:44). The natural self-centered condition of human hearts cannot believe, because they cannot see spiritual beauty. It is not a *physical* inability, as though they can't act even if they have a compelling desire to act. It is a *moral* inability because they are so self-absorbed, they are unable to see what would condemn their pride and give them joy through admiring another. That is why seeing the glory of Christ requires a profound spiritual change.

UNLESS YOU ARE BORN AGAIN YOU CANNOT SEE

So when the disciples do see the glory of Christ and believe in him, Jesus says, "Blessed are your eyes, for they see, and your ears, for they hear" (Matt. 13:16). There is a special work of grace—a special blessedness—that changes our hearts and enables us to see spiritual glory. When Peter said to Jesus, "You are the Christ, the Son of the living God," he had seen the glory of Christ and believed. To this Jesus responded, "Blessed are you, Simon Bar-Jonah! For flesh and blood has not revealed this to you, but my Father who is in heaven" (Matt. 16:16-17).

This is what Jesus meant when he said, "Unless one is born again he cannot see the kingdom of God" (John 3:3). "That which is born of the flesh is flesh, and that which is born of the Spirit is

---

attention on Jesus, trusting completely in him (his power and his love), she would see this miracle as a true sign, an illustration and proof of the glory of God reflected in the Son of God." William Hendriksen, *The Gospel of John* (Edinburgh: Banner of Truth, 1954), 158.

[18] "One might charitably hope that the motive of at least some of them was to win the Pharisees to the truth, but the contrast set up between those who believe and those who go to the Pharisees suggests that their intent was more malicious." D. A. Carson, *The Gospel According to John* (Grand Rapids, Mich.: Eerdmans, 1991), 419.

spirit" (John 3:6). When we are born again by the Spirit of God, our spirits are made alive, and we are able to perceive self-authenticating spiritual beauty in the person and work of Christ.[19]

Seeing the Glory of Christ Has Its Ups and Downs

The ability to see spiritual beauty is not unwavering. There are ups and downs in our fellowship with Christ. There are times of beclouded vision, especially if sin gets the upper hand in our lives for a season. "Blessed are the pure in heart, for they shall see God" (Matt. 5:8). Yes, and this is not an all-or-nothing reality. There are degrees of purity and degrees of seeing. Only when we are perfected in the age to come will our seeing be totally unclouded. "For now we see in a mirror dimly, but then face to face. Now I know in part; then I shall know fully, even as I have been fully known" (1 Cor. 13:12).

This is why Paul prayed the way he did for the believers of Ephesus. "[May God] give you a spirit of wisdom and of revelation in the knowledge of him, having *the eyes of your hearts enlightened*, that you may know what is the hope to which he has called you, what are the riches of his glorious inheritance in the saints, and what is the immeasurable greatness of his power toward us who believe" (Eph. 1:17-19). Notice Paul's distinction between the eyes of the head and the eyes of the heart. There is a heart-seeing, not just a head-seeing. There is a spiritual seeing and a physical seeing. And what he longs for us to see spiritually is "the hope to which [God] has called" us, "the riches of his glorious inheritance," and "the immeasurable greatness of his power." In other words, what he wants us to see is the spiritual reality and value of these things, not just raw facts that unbelievers can read and repeat. That is not the point of spiritual seeing. Spiritual seeing is seeing spiritual

---

[19] Additional texts teaching this truth include Luke 10:22, "All things have been handed over to me by my Father, and no one knows who the Son is except the Father, or who the Father is except the Son and anyone to whom the Son chooses to reveal him." John 6:37, "All that the Father gives me will come to me." John 6:44 , "No one can come to me unless the Father who sent me draws him." John 6:65 , "No one can come to me unless it is granted him by the Father." Acts 13:48, "As many as were appointed to eternal life believed."

things for what they really are—that is, seeing them as beautiful and valuable as they really are.

THE MOST GRACIOUS COMMAND AND BEST GIFT OF THE GOSPEL

The ultimate good of the gospel is seeing and savoring the beauty and value of God. God's wrath and our sin obstruct that vision and that pleasure. You can't see and savor God as supremely satisfying while you are full of rebellion against him and he is full of wrath against you. The removal of this wrath and this rebellion is what the gospel is for. The ultimate aim of the gospel is the display of God's glory and the removal of every obstacle to our seeing it and savoring it as our highest treasure. "Behold your God!" is the most gracious command and best gift of the gospel. If we do not see him and savor him as our greatest fortune, we have not obeyed or believed the gospel. There is a passage in the Bible that makes this even more clear than any we have seen. To this we now turn.

In their case the god of this world has blinded the minds of the unbelievers, to keep them from seeing the light of the gospel of the glory of Christ, who is the image of God. . . . For God, who said, "Let light shine out of darkness," has shone in our hearts to give the light of the knowledge of the glory of God in the face of Jesus Christ.

2 CORINTHIANS 4:4-6

4

THE GOSPEL—
THE GLORY OF CHRIST,
THE IMAGE OF GOD

In this chapter we take up the most important biblical text to make clear the point of this book. It is Paul's way of unfolding the meaning of the gospel command, "Behold your God!" (Isa. 40:9). In 2 Corinthians 4:4-6 seeing God's glory in Christ is explicitly identified with the gospel.

> *The god of this world has blinded the minds of the unbelievers, to keep them from seeing[1] the light of the gospel of the glory of Christ, who is the image of God. For what we proclaim is not ourselves, but Jesus Christ as Lord, with ourselves as your servants for Jesus' sake. For God, who said, "Let light shine out of darkness," has shone in our hearts to give the light of the knowledge of the glory of God in the face of Jesus Christ.*

This is one of the most remarkable descriptions of the gospel in the whole Bible. There is nothing else quite like it. It defines the gospel as "the gospel of the glory of Christ." And it says that this gospel of Christ's glory emits, as it were, a "light"—"the light of the gos-

---

[1] The unusual word for "see" (αὐγάσαι) is used only here in the New Testament. It can mean "shine" or "be bright" or "see distinctly." In this context "seeing distinctly" is the proper translation because the god of this age is blinding the mind so that does not happen. But blindness does not stop a light from shining. It stops a light from being *seen*.

pel of the glory of Christ." And it says that Satan does not want us to "see" this light. Seeing "the light of the gospel of the glory of Christ" is what liberates people from his power.

LIBERATOR FROM THE BLINDING WORK OF SATAN

Compare Christ's commission to Paul in sending him out as his apostle. Christ says that he is sending Paul to the Gentiles in order "to open their eyes, so that they may *turn from darkness to light and from the power of Satan to God,* that they may receive forgiveness of sins and a place among those who are sanctified by faith in me" (Acts 26:18). In other words, in the ministry of the gospel through Paul the eyes of the spiritually blind are opened, light dawns in the heart, the power of Satan's darkness is broken, faith is awakened, forgiveness of sins is received, and sanctification begins.[2]

In 2 Corinthians 4:7 Paul describes himself as a jar of clay with a powerful gospel inside: "We have this treasure [the gospel of the glory of Christ] in jars of clay, to show that the surpassing power belongs to God and not to us." His ministry is not to exalt himself. God sees to it that Paul has little ground for boasting—even among men. Afflictions and weaknesses abound (4:8-18). But that is no hindrance to letting the glory of the gospel shine. "For what we proclaim is not ourselves, but Jesus Christ as Lord, with ourselves as your servants for Jesus' sake" (4:5).

LET THERE BE LIGHT!

God uses weak, afflicted clay pots to carry "the surpassing power" of "the light of the gospel of the glory of Christ." What happens

---

[2] Seyoon Kim points out the parallels between Acts 26:16-18 and 2 Corinthians 4:4-6 in *Paul and the New Perspective: Second Thoughts on the Origin of Paul's Gospel* (Grand Rapids, Mich.: Eerdmans, 2002), 102 n. 4. See his following table:

Acts 26:16-18	2 Corinthians 4:4-6
(1) Paul's commission	Paul's commission
(2) vision of God	vision of God
(3) existence under Satan	under "the god of this age"
(4) [blinded—presupposed]	blinded
(5) turning to God	[implied: turning to God; cf. 3:16-18
(ἐπιστρέφειν)	(ἐπιστρέφειν)]
(6) from darkness to light	from darkness to light

when these clay pots preach the gospel and offer themselves as servants? Verse 6 gives the answer: "God, who said, 'Let light shine out of darkness,' has shone in our hearts to give the light of the knowledge of the glory of God in the face of Jesus Christ." This means that in the dark and troubled heart of unbelief, God does what he did in the dark and unformed creation at the beginning of our world. He said, "Let there be light," and there was light. So he says to the blind and dark heart, "Let there be light," and there is light in the heart of the sinner. In this light we see the glory of God in the face of Christ.

Notice the parallels between verses 4 and 6.

Verse 4	*Verse 6*
Satan blinds to	God creates
the light	the light
of the gospel	of the knowledge
of the glory	of the glory
of Christ	of God
who is the image of God	in the face of Christ

In verse 4 Satan blinds the mind; in verse 6 God creates light in the heart. Verse 4 describes the problem; verse 6 describes the remedy. These two verses are a description of the condition of all people before conversion, and what happens in conversion to bring about salvation. More than any part of the Bible that I know of, the connections between 2 Corinthians 4:4 and 6 shed light on the ultimate meaning of *good* in the term *good news*.

THE GOSPEL IS THE GLORY OF CHRIST

Let's be clear that we are talking about the *gospel* in these verses. The fact that Paul does not mention the facts of Christ's life and death and resurrection does not mean he has left them behind. They remain the historical core of the gospel. There is no gospel without the declaration of Christ crucified for sinners and risen from the dead (1 Cor. 15:1-4). This is assumed here. When Paul speaks of "the gospel of the glory of Christ," he means that the events of the gospel are designed by God to reveal the glory of Christ. This is not incidental to the gospel—it's essential. The gospel would not be good news if it did not reveal the glory of Christ for us to see and savor. It is the glory of Christ that finally satisfies our soul. We are made for Christ, and Christ died so that every obstacle would be removed that keeps us from seeing and savoring the most satisfying treasure in the universe—namely, Christ, who is the image of God.

The supreme value of the glory of Christ revealed in the gospel is what makes Satan so furious with the gospel. Satan is not mainly interested in causing us misery. He is mainly interested in making Christ look bad. He hates Christ. And he hates the glory of Christ. He will do all he can to keep people from seeing Christ as glorious. The gospel is God's instrument for liberating people from exulting in self to exulting in Christ. Therefore Satan hates the gospel.

SATAN'S STRATEGIES TO SILENCE THE GOSPEL

Thus 2 Corinthians 4:4 says that Satan blinds people to keep them from seeing "the light of the *gospel*." He has more than one way to do this. One way, of course, is to prevent the preaching of the gospel. This he does by derailing many preachers and missionaries. They may die, or be thrown in prison (Rev. 2:10), or forsake the ministry (2 Tim. 4:10). Or they may abandon the truth and speak "a different gospel" (Gal. 1:6-8; Acts 20:30).

But in 2 Corinthians 4:4 the way Satan keeps people from seeing "the light of the gospel" is not by preventing preaching, but by preventing spiritual perception. The words of the gospel are heard. The facts are comprehended. But there is no "light." What does this mean? It means that blinded persons consider the facts of the gospel but see no compelling spiritual beauty, no treasure, nothing supremely precious. They see facts. They may even agree that the historical facts are true. Satan surely does. But they do not have "true sense of the divine excellency of the things revealed in the Word of God, and a conviction of the truth and reality of them thence arising."[3]

---

[3] Jonathan Edwards, "A Divine and Supernatural Light," in *Sermons and Discourses 1730-1733*, in *The Works of Jonathan Edwards*, vol. 17, ed. Mark Valeri (New Haven, Conn.: Yale University Press, 1999), 413.

That last quote is from Jonathan Edwards. Edwards thought more deeply about this spiritual "light of the gospel" than anyone I have ever read. Here is how he describes what Satan prevents in verse 4, and what God gives in verse 6.

> [It is] a true sense . . . of the excellency of God and Jesus Christ, and of the work of redemption, and the ways and works of God revealed in the gospel. There is a divine and superlative glory in these things, an excellency that is of a vastly higher kind and more sublime nature than in other things, [and] a glory greatly distinguishing them from all that is earthly and temporal. He that is spiritually enlightened truly apprehends and sees it, or has a sense of it. He does not merely rationally believe that God is glorious, but he has a sense of the gloriousness of God in his heart.[4]

TASTE AND SEE BECAUSE TASTING IS SEEING

Seeing this "light of the gospel of the glory of Christ" is not neutral. One cannot see it and hate it. One cannot see it and reject it. If one claims to see it, only to reject it, one is "seeing" it only the way Satan sees it and wants us to see it. In that case we are still in the grip of his blinding power. No, the kind of seeing that Satan prevents is not the neutral seeing that sets you before a meal with no taste or distaste for what you see. The kind of seeing that Satan cancels (v. 4) and God creates (v. 6) is more like spiritual tasting than rational testing.

This kind of seeing is not the circumstantial inference that the brown fluid in the bottle with the wax comb must be honey. Rather this seeing is the immediate knowledge that it is honey because of putting some on the tongue. There is no series of arguments that awakens the certainty of sweetness. This is what seeing light means. If you are blind, someone may persuade you that the sun is bright. But that persuasion is not what Paul is talking about. When your eyes are opened—that is, when God says, "Let there be light"—the persuasion is of a different kind. That's what happens in the preach-

---

[4] Ibid.

ing of the gospel. It's what happens when God moves with Creator power over the darkness of human hearts.

Jonathan Edwards again helps us see these things more clearly:

> There is a twofold understanding or knowledge of good, that God has made the mind of man capable of. The first, that which is merely speculative or notional. . . . The other is that which consists in the sense of the heart: as when there is a sense of the beauty, amiableness, or sweetness of a thing. . . . Thus there is a difference between having an opinion that God is holy and gracious, and having a sense of the loveliness and beauty of that holiness and grace. There is a difference between having a rational judgment that honey is sweet, and having a sense of its sweetness. . . . When the heart is sensible of the beauty and amiableness of a thing, it necessarily feels pleasure in the apprehension. . . . which is a far different thing from having a rational opinion that it is excellent.[5]

Beware of thinking that Edwards is making too much of this spiritual seeing. All these thoughts are not dreamed up. They come from long and earnest meditation on the meaning of the word "light" in 2 Corinthians 4:4 and 6. It is the "light of the gospel" and the "light of . . . knowledge." What must be seen is not mere news and not mere knowledge. What must be seen is *light*. And the light gets its unique quality from the fact that the light of the "gospel of . . . glory" and the light of "the knowledge of . . . glory" are one. The light of the glory of Christ, and the light of the glory of God are one light. They will, in the end, prove to be one glory. But the point here is this: the glory of God in Christ, revealed through the gospel, is a real, objective *light* that must be spiritually seen in order for there to be salvation. If it is not seen—spiritually tasted as glorious and precious—Satan still has his way, and there is no salvation.[6]

---

[5] Ibid., 414.

[6] In the New Testament one of the ways that those who are perishing are distinguished from the saved is by the fact that they have not "seen" God. For example, 1 John 3:6b, "No one who keeps on sinning has either *seen him or known him.*" And 3 John 11, "Whoever does good is from God; whoever does evil *has not seen God.*"

THE GOSPEL REVEALS A GLORIOUS PERSON

Consider further that Paul speaks here of Christ revealing his glory through the gospel. First there is Christ; then there is the revelation of his glory; then there is the revelation of this glory through the gospel. Let's ponder these three steps in turn.

First there is Christ. The glory spoken of in 2 Corinthians 4:4 is not a vague, impersonal glory, like the glory of sunshine. It is the glory of a *person*. Paul speaks of "the light of the gospel of the glory *of Christ*." The treasure in this text is not glory *per se*. It is *Christ in his glory. It is the glorious Christ.* He is the ultimate gift and treasure of the gospel. All other words and deeds are means to this: seeing Jesus Christ—the kind of seeing that is seeing and savoring simultaneously.

Second, there is the revelation of glory—Christ revealing his *glory* through the gospel. We saw earlier (in Chapter 3) that his glory, in his first coming, was the incomparably exquisite array of spiritual, moral, intellectual, verbal, and practical perfections that manifest themselves in a kind of meek miracle-working and unanswerable teaching and humble action that set Jesus apart from all men. Each of Jesus' deeds and words and attitudes was glorious, but it is the way they come together in beautiful summation—I called it an exquisite array—that constitutes his glory.

But the climax of the glory of his life on earth was the way it ended. It was as if all the darker colors in the spectrum of glory came together in the most beautiful sunset on Good Friday, with the crucified Christ as the blood-red sun in the crimson sky. And it was as if all the brighter colors in the spectrum of glory came together in the most beautiful sunrise on Easter morning, with the risen Christ as the golden sun shining in full strength. Both the glory of the sunset and the glory of the sunrise shone on the horizon of a lifetime of incomparably beautiful love. This is what Paul meant in 2 Corinthians 4:4 when he spoke of "the glory of Christ." It is the glory of a person. But the person displays his glory in words and actions and feelings. The glory is not the glory of a painting or even a sunset. Those are only analogies. They are too static and lifeless.

The spiritual beauty of Christ is Christ-in-action—Christ loving, and Christ touching lepers, and Christ blessing children, and healing the crippled, and raising the dead, and commanding demons, and teaching with unrivaled authority, and silencing the skeptics, and rebuking his disciples, and predicting the details of his death, and setting his face like flint toward Jerusalem, and weeping over the city, and silent before his accusers, and meekly sovereign over Pilate ("You would have no authority over me at all unless it had been given you from above," John 19:11), and crucified, and praying for his enemies, and forgiving a thief, and caring for his mother while in agony, and giving up his spirit in death, and rising from the dead— "No one takes [my life] from me, but I lay it down of my own accord. I have authority to lay it down, and I have authority to take it up again" (John 10:18). Such is the glory of Christ.

THIS IS THE GOSPEL: THE REVELATION OF THE GLORY OF GOD IN CHRIST

Third, there is the gospel—Christ revealing his glory *through the gospel*. The gospel is good news. It is the proclamation of what happened. The first generation of disciples saw these happenings with their own eyes. But for all of us since then, the glory of Christ is mediated through their proclamation. This is the way they said it would be: "That which was from the beginning, which we have heard, which we have seen with our eyes, which we looked upon and have touched with our hands, concerning the word of life . . . that which we have seen and heard we proclaim also to you" (1 John 1:1-3).

The glorious person who once walked the earth is now unseen. All his decisive acts are in the invisible past. We do not have any videos or recordings of Jesus Christ on earth. What we have linking us with Christ and with his cross and resurrection is the word of God, and its center, the gospel. "O foolish Galatians! Who has bewitched you? It was before your eyes that Jesus Christ was publicly portrayed as crucified" (Galatians 3:1). God has ordained that the true, flesh-and-blood reality of Christ carry across the centuries by means of the Scriptures—and their blazing center, the gospel of Christ crucified and risen.

This is how Paul defined the center of the gospel: "Christ died for our sins in accordance with the Scriptures . . . he was buried . . . he was raised on the third day in accordance with the Scriptures" (1 Cor. 15:3-4). These are the indispensable deeds of the gospel. Other things are implied, even essential, but these are explicit and essential.

His death and resurrection are where the glory of Christ shines most brightly. There is a divine glory in the way Jesus embraced his death and what he accomplished by it. So Paul says, "We preach Christ crucified, a stumbling block to Jews and folly to Gentiles, but to those who are called, both Jews and Greeks, *Christ the power of God and the wisdom of God*" (1 Cor. 1:23-24). "The word of the cross is folly to those who are perishing, but to us who are being saved it is the power of God" (1 Cor. 1:18). For those who have eyes to see, there is divine glory in the death of Jesus.

So it is with his resurrection. Paul said that when the human body dies it "is sown in dishonor" and when it is raised "it is raised in glory" (1 Cor. 15:43). It was the glory of God that raised Jesus, and it was the glory of God into which he was raised: He was "raised from the dead by the glory of the Father" (Rom. 6:4), and then the Father "gave him glory" (1 Pet. 1:21). Jesus himself said after he was raised, "Was it not necessary that the Christ should suffer these things and enter into his glory?" (Luke 24:26).

Therefore, when the gospel is preached in its fullness, and by God's mighty grace Satan's blinding power is overcome, and God says to the human soul, "Let there be light!" what the soul sees and savors in the gospel is "the light of the gospel of the glory of Christ." That is the aim of gospel preaching.

THIS GLORY OF CHRIST IS THE GLORY OF GOD

The glory of Christ, which we see in the gospel, is *God's* glory for at least three reasons. The first is that God speaks the light of the glory into being in our hearts. Second Corinthians 4:6 makes this clear:

"God, who said, 'Let light shine out of darkness,' has shone in our hearts to give the light of the knowledge of the glory of God in the face of Jesus Christ." Two times the verse says that God created the light: the first one referring to the creation of this world ("God, who said, 'Let light shine out of darkness'"), and the second one referring to the creation of light in our hearts ("has shone in our hearts to give the light"). Therefore this is God's light. He creates it. He gives it.

But we must not make the mistake of thinking that because God creates the light in our hearts, it is not the objective light of the glory of the events of Good Friday and Easter. Paul is not saying that God creates light in the heart apart from the gospel events. No, the light God creates is "the light of the gospel of the glory of Christ." It is not an independent or different light from what Christ revealed in history. When this light shines in the soul by God's sovereign creation, what the soul sees is the glory of Christ acting in the gospel.

So we must hold fast to two truths, not just one, even if they seem to be in tension. First, we must hold fast to the truth that the spiritual light Paul speaks about in verse 4 actually streams from the events of the gospel of Christ. The other truth is that God creates this light in the heart. It is not caused by human preaching. It is caused immediately by God. Here is the way Jonathan Edwards describes these two truths:

> This light is immediately given by God, and not obtained by natural means. . . . 'Tis not in this affair, as it is in inspiration [of the Scriptures], where new truths are suggested; for there is by this light only given a due apprehension of the same truths that are revealed in the Word of God; and therefore it is not given without the Word. . . . The word of God . . . conveys to our minds these and those doctrines; it is the cause of the notion of them in our heads, but not the sense of the divine excellency of them in our hearts. Indeed a person can't have spiritual light without the Word. . . . As for instance, that notion that there is a Christ, and that Christ is holy and gracious, is conveyed to the mind by the Word of God: but the sense of the excel-

lency of Christ by reason of that holiness and grace, is nevertheless immediately the work of the Holy Spirit.[7]

So the light of the glory of Christ that shines through the gospel is the light of God's glory. And the first reason is that God himself speaks the light of that glory into being in our hearts.

THE GLORY OF CHRIST IS THE GLORY OF GOD IN THE FACE OF CHRIST

The second reason that the glory of Christ is the glory of God is that Christ is the image of God. Paul says this explicitly in verse 4 and then differently in verse 6. In verse 4 he refers to "the light of the gospel of the glory of Christ, *who is the image of God.*" And in verse 6 he refers to "the light of the knowledge of the glory of God *in the face of Jesus Christ.*" Thus he shows that the glory is one glory by saying it in two ways. First, it is the glory of Christ, but Christ is "the image of God," and so it is also the glory of God. Or again, it is the glory of God, but it is "in the face of Jesus Christ," so it is also the glory of Christ.

The reference to "the face of Jesus Christ" (v. 6) is remarkable. God "has shone in our hearts to give the light of the knowledge of the glory of God *in the face of Jesus Christ.*" Combined with the word "image" in verse 4, the emphasis seems to be on visibility, openness, knowability.[8] God must have an image to be seen. Or another way to say it is that God must have a human face. That image is Christ, and that face is the face of Christ. But the seeing is not the seeing of photography or video. It is the seeing that can

---

[7] Edwards, "A Divine and Supernatural Light," 416-417.

[8] Several verses before 2 Corinthians 4:4-6 Paul had spoken of another face, namely, Moses'. Paul pointed out that what Moses had seen on Mount Sinai made his face radiant with glory. But this was a fading glory, and Moses would cover his face so that the fading glory would not be seen. "The Israelites could not gaze at Moses' face because of its glory, which was being brought to an end . . . [So Moses] put a veil over his face so that the Israelites might not gaze at the outcome of what was being brought to an end" (2 Cor. 3:7, 13). But Paul said that the glory of Christ in the new covenant would not be a fading glory. "For if what was being brought to an end came with glory, much more will what is permanent have glory" (2 Cor. 3:11). So it makes sense that Paul would refer to the "face of Jesus Christ" since he is contrasting the ministry of Christ with the ministry of Moses whose face had to be veiled.

happen through the Word and by the Spirit. Jesus did have a literal, physical, human face. That is implied and important. The glory of God shone in the historical, bodily face of Jesus.

His face was the brightness of his person. If you want to know a person, you don't look mainly at his neck or shoulder or knee. You look at his face. The face is the window on the soul. The face is the revelation of the heart. The face carries the emotions of joy or sadness or anger or grief. We have words like *smile* and *frown* to express how the heart is manifest in the face. We do not smile or frown with the wrist or the knee. The face represents the person in direct communication. If someone hides his face from us, he does not want to be known. The real, bodily face of Jesus matters. It signifies that he was a real human being and that he was a person revealed in real, historical, physical life.

THE FUTURE FACE OF CHRIST

This is also important because Jesus was raised from the dead with that same bodily face. Our hope for future fellowship with him is not hope for a ghost-like floating in the same vicinity. It is the hope to see him face to face. Paul said this in words that would anticipate this passage: "Now we see in a mirror dimly, but then *face to face*. Now I know in part; then I shall know fully, even as I have been fully known" (1 Corinthians 13:12). If we see dimly now and later hope to see face to face, then what we are seeing dimly now is "the face of Jesus Christ." That is, we are seeing the glory of the real historical person manifest in words and deeds and feelings as he really was in the body on this earth.

This is what we hope to see when he returns, and it is what Paul says those who do not believe will lose: "They will suffer the punishment of eternal destruction, *away from* the presence [literally: face] of the Lord and from the glory of his might" (2 Thess. 1:9). But those who believe will "marvel" and "glory" at the face of Christ when he returns (2 Thess. 1:10). We will not be satisfied until the day when we look on Jesus face to face. A real face. A human face. But oh, so much more! A face infinitely radiant with the glory of his might.

THE DEEPEST REASON WHY CHRIST'S GLORY IS GOD'S GLORY

Implicit in what we have said so far about the glory of Christ being the glory of God is that Christ and God are one in essence. They are both God. But we should make this explicit now because its relevance for the meaning of the gospel in 2 Corinthians 4:4-6 is huge. The third reason that the glory of Christ is the glory of God is that Christ is God.[9]

Jesus Christ "is the radiance of the glory of God and the exact imprint of his nature" (Heb. 1:3). "The Word became flesh and dwelt among us, and we have seen his glory, glory as of the only Son from the Father" (John 1:14). This was not the glory of a creature. This is the glory of a begotten Son—begotten from all eternity, as implied in John 1:1, "In the beginning was the Word, and the Word was with God, and the Word was God." His glory is the glory of God because Jesus Christ is God. The glory of the only Son—not the creature-sons, like us, but the divine Son—is the glory of the Father because they are of the same essence, the same divine Being.[10] "In him the whole fullness of deity dwells bodily" (Col. 2:9; see 1:19). This is the fullest reason why he is called "the image of the invisible God" (Col. 1:15). It is also the fullest reason why Jesus said, "I and the Father are one" (John 10:30), and, "Whoever has seen me has seen the Father" (John 14:9), and, "The Father is in me and I am in the Father" (John 10:38), and, "I am the Alpha and the Omega, the first and the last, the beginning and the end" (Rev. 22:13).[11]

The glory of Christ is the one glory that all his people are

---

[9] For an excellent and readable introduction to the doctrine of the Trinity (the deity of the Father, the Son, and the Spirit as one God yet three Persons) see Bruce Ware, *Father, Son, and Holy Spirit: Relationships, Roles, and Relevance* (Wheaton, Ill.: Crossway Books, 2005). For a historical overview of the doctrine see Robert Letham, *The Holy Trinity: In Scripture, History, Theology, and Worship* (Phillipsburg, N.J.: P&R, 2004). For a banquet of biblical reflection see Jonathan Edwards, *Writings on the Trinity, Grace, and Faith*, in *The Works of Jonathan Edwards*, ed. Sang Hyun Lee, vol. 21 (New Haven, Conn.: Yale University Press, 2003).

[10] For some of my reflections on the oneness of the Father and the Son see "The Pleasure of God in His Son," in John Piper, *The Pleasures of God: Meditations on God's Delight in Being God* (Sisters, Ore.: Multnomah, 2000), 25-45.

[11] "The attributes expressed in these words are attributed to God himself in [Revelation] 1:8 and 21:6. Christ can be the judge of men because he transcends all human experience, sharing the eternal nature of God himself." George Ladd, *A Commentary on the Revelation of John* (Grand Rapids, Mich.: Eerdmans, 1972), 293.

waiting for—"our blessed hope, the appearing of the glory of our great God and Savior Jesus Christ" (Tit. 2:13). Jesus is "our great God." There is a glory of the Father and a glory of the Son, but they are so united that if you see the one, you see the other. They do not have the same roles in the work of redemption, but the glory manifest in each of their roles shines from them both. No one knows the glory of the Son and is a stranger to the glory of the Father. And no one knows the glory of the Father and is a stranger to the glory of the Son.

KNOWING THE SON MEANS KNOWING THE FATHER

Only the Son and the Father have the capacity to know each other fully, since they have a wholly unique essence—they are God. Therefore, we cannot know them truly if it is not granted to us by a special work of grace. God the Spirit, in the service of the glory of God the Son (John 16:14), grants us the spiritual capacity to know God the Father (John 3:6-8). Because of that new capacity to know God, the Son takes his divine prerogative to make the Father known to us. Thus Jesus says, "No one knows the Son except the Father, and no one knows the Father except the Son and anyone to whom the Son chooses to reveal him" (Matt. 11:27). If the Son chooses to reveal the Father to us, then we have fellowship with both the Father and the Son through the life-giving Spirit. In this fellowship we enjoy seeing and savoring the glory of the Father and the Son.

The Father and the Son are so inseparably one in glory and essence that knowing one implies knowing the other, and loving one implies loving the other. "Whoever confesses that Jesus is the Son of God, God abides in him, and he in God" (1 John 4:15). Confessing Christ, the Son of God, results in God the Father's coming to us and manifesting himself to us. The Father and the Son are so united that to have the one is to have the other. "No one who denies the Son has the Father. Whoever confesses the Son has the Father also" (1 John 2:23). "Everyone who goes on ahead and does not abide in the teaching of Christ, does not have God. Whoever abides in the teaching has both the Father and the Son" (2 John 9).

There is no possibility of knowing God or having a saving relationship with God without knowing and trusting the Son. This is made clear over and over—both negatively and positively. "Whoever does not honor the Son does not honor the Father who sent him" (John 5:23). "Whoever hates me hates my Father also" (John 15:23). "If you knew me, you would know my Father also" (John 8:19). "Whoever receives me receives him who sent me" (Matt. 10:40). "The one who hears you hears me, and the one who rejects you rejects me, and the one who rejects me rejects him who sent me" (Luke 10:16).

THE GOSPEL IS NOT GOOD NEWS WITHOUT THE GLORY OF GOD

The implications of this for understanding 2 Corinthians 4:4-6 are enormous. "The gospel of the glory of Christ" is the gospel of the glory of God, for Christ is God. To see the glory of the work of Christ in the events of Good Friday and Easter is to see the glory of God. To love Christ for his saving work in the gospel is to love God. I am not collapsing all distinctions between the Father and the Son. Rather I am contending against all separation. I am arguing that it is not only permissible but essential to see and savor God in the glory of the gospel. That is the emphasis of 2 Corinthians 4:4, 6, and that is the aim of this book and why I titled it *God Is the Gospel.*

The gospel is the light of the glory of Christ *who is the image of God.* It is the light of the glory of God *in the face of Christ.* This is what makes the gospel good news. If the glory of God in Christ were not given to us in the gospel for our everlasting seeing and savoring, the gospel would not be good news. The emphasis could not be clearer in these verses. In wakening our souls to see and savor the glory of the gospel, Paul emphasizes above all things in these verses that the gospel gives the *glory of God* for us to see and enjoy forever.

"THEY DO NOT SEE THE MIDDAY SUN"

And let us not fail to see the sun at broad day. We are talking about *glory*—radiance, effulgence, brightness. Glory is the outshining of

[margin handwritten note: Key for Mormons]

whatever is glorious. The glory of God is the beautiful brightness of God. There is no greater brightness. Nothing in the universe, nor in the imagination of any man or angel, is brighter than the brightness of God. This makes the blindness of 2 Corinthians 4:4 shocking in its effect. Calvin says it with the kind of amazement it deserves: "They do not see the midday sun."[12] That is how plain the glory of God is in the gospel. When God declares the omnipotent word of creation and "[shines] in our hearts to give the light of the knowledge of the glory of God in the face of Jesus Christ," the curtains are pulled back in the window of our Alpine chalet, and the morning sun, reflected off the Alps of Christ, fills the room with glory.

---

[12] John Calvin, *The Second Epistle of Paul the Apostle to the Corinthians*, trans. T. A. Smail (Grand Rapids, Mich.: Eerdmans, 1964), 53.

The Spirit is the one who testifies, because the Spirit is the truth. . . . If we receive the testimony of men, the testimony of God is greater, for this is the testimony of God that he has borne concerning his Son. . . . And this is the testimony, that God gave us eternal life, and this life is in his Son.

1 JOHN 5:6-11

THE GOSPEL—CONFIRMED BY ITS GLORY, THE INTERNAL TESTIMONY OF THE HOLY SPIRIT

THE GLORY OF GOD IN THE GOSPEL AND THE INTERNAL TESTIMONY OF THE SPIRIT

The glory of God in the gospel is vastly important in ways we may not at first realize. For example, the glory of God in the gospel gives self-authenticating validity and power to the word of the gospel, even for the simplest person. How does a person come to a settled and unshakable faith in the gospel of Christ? For millions of ordinary people over the centuries, who had no access to the intellectual arguments of apologetics, the gospel has been the pathway to sure, well-grounded, unshakable trust in Christ. How can this be? What is the foundation of such faith? Is it not the revelation in the gospel of the self-authenticating "glory of God in the face of Jesus Christ"? Pondering this question in relation to the historic doctrine of the internal testimony of the Holy Spirit will shed even more light on the preciousness and beauty of the truth that the glory of God is the ultimate brightness of the gospel.

FAITH FROM THE TESTIMONY OF THE SPIRIT IS NOT IRRATIONAL

The revelation of the majesty of the glory of God in the gospel is one reason why it is not irrational or arbitrary to believe the gospel because of the internal testimony of the Holy Spirit. Sometimes when we hear that the Holy Spirit enables us to believe the gospel, or that the Spirit bears witness to the truth of the gospel, we have the notion in our minds that the validity of the gospel depends on new information given by the Spirit. But that is not what is meant historically by the internal testimony of the Spirit. We can see this from the way John Calvin[1] and Jonathan Edwards thought about this matter.

NOT THE CHURCH BUT THE SPIRIT CONFIRMS THE WORD

As John Calvin pondered the basis of our confidence in the gospel, he was dismayed that the Roman Catholic Church made the authority of the Word dependent on the authority of the church:

> A most pernicious error widely prevails that Scripture has only so much weight as is conceded to it by the consent of the church. As if the eternal and inviolable truth of God depended upon the decision of men! . . . Yet, if this is so, what will happen to miserable consciences seeking firm assurance of eternal life if all promises of it consist in and depend solely upon the judgment of men?[2]

How then shall we know for sure that the gospel is the word of God? How shall we be sure, not just that these things happened, but that the biblical meaning given to the great events of the gospel is the true meaning—God's meaning? Calvin continues:

> The testimony of the Spirit is more excellent than all reason. For as God alone is a fit witness of himself in his Word, so also the Word will not find acceptance in men's hearts before it is sealed by the inward testimony of the Spirit. The same Spirit therefore who has spoken through the mouths of the prophets must penetrate into our

---

[1] In what follows I am leaning on what I wrote in "The Divine Majesty of the Word," in *The Legacy of Sovereign Joy* (Wheaton, Ill.: Crossway Books, 2000), 115-142.
[2] John Calvin, *Institutes of the Christian Religion*, 2 vols., ed. John T. McNeill, trans. Ford Lewis Battles (Philadelphia: Westminster Press, 1960), 1:75 (I.vii.1).

hearts to persuade us that they faithfully proclaimed what had been divinely commanded . . . because until he illumines their minds, they ever waver among many doubts![3]

THE UNMISTAKABLE MAJESTY OF GOD MANIFEST IN THE WORD

But how does this persuasion happen? Is it by the Spirit telling us a new fact—namely, the whisper, "This book is true"? Do we hear a voice? That is not the way it happens. The glory of God in the gospel does not need another witness of that sort. How then does the internal testimony of the Spirit work in conjunction with the glory of God in the gospel? What does the Spirit do?

The answer is not that the Spirit gives us added revelation to what is in Scripture, but that he awakens us, as from the dead, to see and taste the divine reality of the glory of Christ in the gospel. (Recall the seeing of 2 Corinthians 4:4, 6.) This sight authenticates the gospel as God's own word. Calvin says, "Our Heavenly Father, revealing his majesty [in the gospel], lifts reverence for Scripture beyond the realm of controversy."[4] This is the key for Calvin: the witness of God to the gospel is the immediate, unassailable, life-giving revelation to the mind of the majesty of God manifest in the Word itself—not in new revelation about it.

We are almost at the bottom of this experience of the internal testimony of the Spirit. Here are the words that will take us deeper.

> Therefore illumined by [the Spirit's] power, we believe neither by our own [*note this!*] nor by anyone else's judgment that Scripture is from God; but above human judgment we affirm with utter certainty (just as if we were gazing upon the majesty of God himself) that it has flowed to us from the very mouth of God by the ministry of men.[5]

---

[3] Ibid., 79 (I.vii.4).
[4] Ibid., 92 (I.viii.13).
[5] Ibid., 80 (I.vii.5).

GOD'S TESTIMONY IS THE GIFT OF LIFE, AND THEREFORE SIGHT

This is almost baffling. He says that his conviction concerning the majesty of God in Scripture—that is, the glory of God in the gospel—rests not in any human judgment, not even his own. What does he mean? As I have wrestled with this, the words of the apostle John have shed the most helpful light on what Calvin is trying to explain. Here are the key words from 1 John 5:6-11:

> *The Spirit is the one who testifies, because the Spirit is the truth. . . . If we receive the testimony of men, the testimony of God [= the Spirit] is greater, for this is the testimony of God that he has borne concerning his Son. . . . And this is the testimony, that God gave us eternal life, and this life is in his Son.*

In other words, "the testimony of God," that is, the inward witness of the Spirit, is greater than any human witness—including, I think the apostle would say in this context, the witness of our own judgment. And what is that testimony of God? It is not merely a word delivered to our judgment for reflection, for then our conviction would rely on our own reflection. What is it then? Verse 11 is the key: "This is the testimony, that God gave us eternal life." I take that to mean that God testifies to us of his reality and the reality of his Son and of the gospel by giving us life from the dead, so that we come alive to his self-authenticating glory in the gospel. In that instant we do not reason from premises to conclusions; rather we see that we are awake, and there is not even a prior human judgment about it to lean on. When Lazarus wakened in the tomb by the call or the "testimony" of Christ, he knew without reasoning that he was alive and that this call awakened him.

So when Calvin was asked, "How can we be assured that [the gospel] has sprung from God unless we have recourse to the decree of the church?" he responded in amazement, "It is as if someone asked: Whence will we learn to distinguish light from darkness, white from black, sweet from bitter? Indeed, Scripture exhibits fully as clear evidence of its own truth as white and black things do of their color, or sweet and bitter things do of their taste."[6]

THE GOD-EXALTING GOSPEL IS SELF-AUTHENTICATING

So the internal testimony of the Holy Spirit, which persuades us that the gospel is true, is not the adding of new information to what is in the gospel. Rather it is the same as what Paul describes in 2 Corinthians 4:6, "For God, who said, 'Let light shine out of darkness,' has shone in our hearts to give the light of the knowledge of the glory of God in the face of Jesus Christ." In other words, by the Spirit we are enabled to see what is really there in the gospel. There is real light and real glory, and it is manifestly divine. It carries its own authentication. Here's the way J. I. Packer puts it:

> Calvin affirms Scripture to be self-authenticating through the inner witness of the Holy Spirit. What is this 'inner witness'? Not a special quality of experience, nor a new, private revelation, nor an existential 'decision', but a work of enlightenment whereby, through the medium of verbal testimony, the blind eyes of the spirit are opened, and divine realities come to be recognized and embraced for what they are. This recognition Calvin says, is as immediate and unanalysable as the perceiving of a color, or a taste, by physical sense—an event about which no more can be said than that when appropriate stimuli were present it happened, and when it happened we know it had happened.[7]

Therefore the doctrine of the internal testimony of the Spirit is valid because the gospel is a revelation of the glory of Christ who is the image of God. If we minimize the majesty of God as the greatest good in the good news, we strip from the gospel the all-important ground of saving faith. This becomes even more clear as we ponder the way Jonathan Edwards wrestled with the question of how people—especially ordinary, uneducated people, like the Indians on

---

[6] Ibid., 76 (I.vii.2).

[7] J. I. Packer, "Calvin the Theologian," in *John Calvin: A Collection of Essays* (Grand Rapids, Mich.: Eerdmans, 1966), 166.

the New England frontier—could have unshakable faith that would even suffer martyrdom.

THE GROUND OF OUR FAITH MUST BE REASONABLE

Jonathan Edwards shared Calvin's conviction about the ground of our faith in the gospel. It is the glory of God seen with the eyes of the heart as majestic and self-authenticating. But Edwards strikes a slightly different note. He stresses that the conviction of the truth of the gospel must be both *reasonable* and *spiritual*. The glory of God in the gospel is the key to both.

Edwards says that even if a person has strong religious affections that arise from a persuasion of the truth of the gospel, these affections are worthless "unless their persuasion be a *reasonable* persuasion or conviction."[8] What does he mean by "reasonable"?

> By a reasonable conviction, I mean, a conviction founded on real evidence, or upon that which is a good reason, or just ground of conviction. Men may have a strong persuasion that the Christian religion is true, when their persuasion is not at all built on evidence, but altogether on education, and the opinion of others; as many Mahometans are strongly persuaded of the truth of the Mahometan religion,[9] because their fathers, and neighbors, and nation believe it. That belief of the truth of the Christian religion, which is built on the very same grounds with a Mahometan's belief of the Mahometan religion, is the same sort of belief. And though the thing believed happens to be better, yet that does not make the belief itself to be of a better sort; for though the thing believed happens to be true, yet the belief of it is not owing to this truth, but to education. So that as the conviction is no better than the Mahometan's conviction; so the affections that flow from it, are no better in themselves, than the religious affections of Mahometans.[10]

One of my main concerns in writing this book is that many people profess faith in Christ in this way. It is not a faith founded on

---

[8] Jonathan Edwards, *Religious Affections*, in *The Works of Jonathan Edwards*, ed. John E. Smith, vol. 2 (New Haven, Conn.: Yale University Press, 1959), 295.
[9] "Mahometan" is an archaic term for a Muslim.
[10] Edwards, *Religious Affections*, 295.

the glory of Christ himself but on tradition or education or other people's opinion. If that is the case, the faith is not saving faith. Saving faith in Christ is built, as Edwards says, upon "real evidence, or upon that which is a good reason, or just ground of conviction."

THE REASONABLE GROUND OF FAITH MUST BE SPIRITUAL

But what is that "good reason" or "just ground" upon which faith must be based? The answer to this question also defines what he means by a true conviction being "spiritual." For faith and its fruit to be truly "gracious," that is, saving, Edwards says, "It is requisite, not only that the belief . . . should be a *reasonable*, but also a *spiritual* belief or conviction."[11] He says this because the "good reason" and "just ground" of conviction must arise from a spiritual—that is, Spirit-enabled—sight of the glory of God in the gospel.

> A *spiritual* conviction of the truth of the great things of the gospel, is such a conviction, as arises from having a spiritual view or apprehension of those things in the mind. And this is also evident from the Scripture, which often represents, that a saving belief of the reality and divinity of the things proposed and exhibited to us in the gospel, is from the Spirit of God's enlightening the mind.[12]

Then, to support this, Edwards cites the text that we were concerned with in the previous chapter, 2 Corinthians 4:4-6, especially verse 6 ("[God] has shone in our hearts to give the light of the knowledge of the glory of God in the face of Jesus Christ"). Then he comments on this verse: "Nothing can be more evident, than that a saving belief of the gospel is here spoken of, by the apostle, as arising from the mind's being enlightened to behold the divine glory of the things it exhibits."[13]

---

[11] Ibid.
[12] Ibid., 296.
[13] Ibid., 298.

GOD'S GLORY IS WHAT THE GOSPEL EVENTS AND PROMISES ARE MEANT TO SHOW

Thus both John Calvin and Jonathan Edwards emphasize that saving faith in the gospel must be based on Spirit-enabled seeing of the glory of God in the face of Christ. I believe they are making clear what 2 Corinthians 4:4-6, and numerous other texts,[14] teach. Therefore, the glory of God in the face of Christ—that is, the glory of Christ who is the image of God—is essential to the gospel. It is not marginal or dispensable. Paul calls the gospel "the gospel of the glory of Christ." This glory is what the events of the gospel are designed to reveal. If a person comes to the gospel and sees the events of Good Friday and Easter and believes that they happened and that they can bring some peace of mind, but does not see and savor any of this divine glory, that person does not have saving faith.

Seeing the glory of God in Christ in the gospel is essential to conversion. Edwards presses this with all his might as he struggles with the painful pastoral fact of false conversions. A professing Christian can have many right words but no spiritual fruit. What is wrong? The supernatural change from darkness to light has not happened. The blinding effects of sin and Satan have not been lifted. The eyes of the heart are still unable to see and savor the glory of Christ who is the image of God.

> When men are converted, they are, as it were, called out of one region into the other, out of a region of darkness into the land of light. . . . In conversion they are brought to see spiritual objects. Those things which before they only heard of by the hearing of the ear, they now are brought to a sight of: a sight of God, and a sight of Christ, and a sight of sin and holiness, a sight of the way of salvation, a sight of the spiritual and invisible world, a sight of the happiness of the enjoyment of God and his favor, and a sight of the dreadfulness of his anger. . . . They are now convinced of the

[14] For example, Edwards cites Luke 10:21-22; John 6:40; 17:6-8; Matthew 16:16-17; Galatians 1:14-16. Ibid., 297.

being of God, after another manner than ever they were before. . . .
'Tis not merely by ratiocination[15] that those things are confirmed
to them; but they are convinced that they are, because that they see
them to be.[16]

Now let us emphasize—since it is the theme of this book—that
these essential, divine things are seen *in the gospel*. It is true that *all*
the Scripture has the mark of God's glory on it, since he is its theme
and author. But in the gospel events of Christ's crucifixion and resurrection—the terrible and wonderful events of Good Friday and
Easter—the glory of God shines most brightly. Thus it is especially
important that we think of the gospel in terms of the revelation of
God's glory. God designed it to be the *main* place where his glory
would be revealed from age to age. Thus Jonathan Edwards says,
"Now this distinguishing glory of the divine Being has its brightest
appearance and manifestation, in the things proposed and exhib-
ited to us in *the gospel,* the doctrines there taught, the word there
spoken, and the divine counsels, acts and works there revealed."[17]

The importance of seeing the glory of Christ in the gospel will
become clearer and more urgent if we ponder how this truth affects
the task of evangelism and missions and the manifold ministries of
the church in trying to change people's behavior. That is what the
next chapter is about.

---

[15] ". . . not that [a person] judges the doctrines of the gospel to be from God, without any argument or deduction at all; but it is without any long chain of arguments; the argument is but
one, and the evidence direct; the mind ascends to the truth of the gospel but by one step, and
that is its divine glory." Ibid., 298.

[16] Jonathan Edwards, "Christians a Chosen Generation," in *Sermons and Discourses 1730-
1733,* in *The Works of Jonathan Edwards,* vol. 17, ed. Mark Valeri (New Haven, Conn.: Yale
University Press, 1999), 322.

[17] Edwards, *Religious Affections,* 300. Emphasis added.

I am sending you to open their eyes, so that they may turn from darkness to light and from the power of Satan to God, that they may receive for-giveness of sins and a place among those who are sanctified by faith in me.

And we all, with unveiled face, beholding the glory of the Lord, are being transformed into the same image from one degree of glory to another. For this comes from the Lord who is the Spirit.

2 CORINTHIANS 3:18

6

THE GOSPEL—THE GLORY OF CHRIST IN EVANGELISM, MISSIONS, AND SANCTIFICATION

The gospel is the revelation of the glory of Christ who is the image of God. It is the self-authenticating display of the light of the knowledge of the glory of God in the face of Christ. The greatest good in the gospel is the gift of seeing and savoring the glory of God in Christ forever. This is supremely important if we would use the gospel biblically in evangelism, missions, and the ministry of the church to sanctify the saints. The holiness of Christian people and the conversion of perishing people hang on seeing and savoring the glory of God in the gospel.

EDWARDS'S BURDEN FOR ILLITERATE UNBELIEVERS

Few minds have surpassed the mind of Jonathan Edwards in greatness of mental vigor and creativity and insight and comprehensiveness. But Edwards had a huge burden for ordinary people in New England, and for Indians on the frontier, and for "Mahometans" across the seas. He points out that these people simply will not be able to come to real, well-grounded faith in the gospel (described in the previous chapter) if they cannot come by a spiritual perception of the self-authenticating glory of God in it.

Unless men may come to a reasonable solid persuasion and conviction of the truth of the gospel, by the internal evidences of it, in the
way that has been spoken, viz. *by a sight of its glory*; 'tis impossible
that those who are illiterate, and unacquainted with history, should
have any thorough and effectual conviction of it at all.[1]

Edwards presses on further as he considers how few people
come to faith through academic arguments for the historical validity of the Bible:

But the gospel was not given only for learned men. There are at least
nineteen in twenty, if not ninety-nine in an hundred, of those for
whom the Scriptures were written, that are not capable of any certain
or effectual conviction of the divine authority of the Scriptures, by
such arguments as learned men make use of.[2]

And how much worse off are those who "have been brought up
on heathenism" and have no knowledge of the history of the world,
let alone of the Bible. If we believe that true conviction and spiritual
certainty must wait for historical argument, this "will render the
propagation of the gospel among them, infinitely difficult."[3]

THE KIND OF FAITH THAT SURVIVES TORTURE
IS NOT BASED ON PROBABILITIES

And even if people can come to a sense of strong probability that
the gospel is true on the basis of historical reasonings, this will not
suffice for sustaining a person in suffering and torture. In centuries
gone by, there have been many suffering saints, including women
and children with little or no education, who lived in times of great
spiritual darkness. Yet how wonderful are the stories of how they
gave themselves up to death. In view of these thousands of saints of
whom the world was not worthy, Edwards observes:

[1] Jonathan Edwards, *Religious Affections*, in *The Works of Jonathan Edwards*, ed. John E.
Smith, vol. 2 (New Haven, Conn.: Yale University Press, 1959), 303.
[2] Ibid., 304.
[3] Ibid.

To have a conviction, so clear, and evident, and assuring, as to be sufficient to induce them, with boldness to sell all, confidently and fearlessly to run the venture of the loss of all things, and of enduring the most exquisite and long continued torments, and to trample the world under foot, and count all things but dung for Christ, the evidence they can have from history, cannot be sufficient. . . . After all that learned men have said to them, there will remain innumerable doubts on their minds; they will be ready, when pinched with some great trial of their faith, to say, "How do I know this, or that? How do I know when these histories were written?" . . . Endless doubts and scruples [will] remain.[4]

Therefore it is crucial for evangelism and missions that we understand that true saving faith is grounded on a spiritual sight of the glory of God in the gospel. This will have a huge impact on the way we think about missions and evangelism. The primary impact will be to make sure that the missionary and the evangelist are spiritual people who see and savor the glory of God in the face of Christ.

TELL THE OLD, OLD STORY AND PRAY FOR THE SPIRIT

Of course, this does not mean that we will not tell the old, old story. We will tell it often and tell it well. The center of the gospel is the narration of the events of Christ's death and resurrection. It is news! Then there is the explanation of what this death and resurrection have achieved in the forgiveness of sins and the hope of eternal life. And in all of this there is the aim and prayer that the glory of Christ would shine through, because this glory is what must be seen in order for faith to have a solid and saving ground. The Holy Spirit must do his life-giving, eye-opening, blindness-removing, glory-revealing work. The Spirit and the Word are both essential. The story of Christ must be told, and the Spirit of Christ must be triumphant. We will see in what follows why the Spirit does not do his saving work without the preaching of the gospel.

---

[4] Ibid., 303.

BEHOLDING THE GLORY OF CHRIST IN THE GOSPEL
FOR THE SAKE OF BECOMING HOLY

The gospel is central not only in conversion but also in the ongoing transformation of believers. Understanding the decisive purpose of the gospel as the revelation of the glory of Christ is the biblical key to Christian holiness. This is made clear in the context of 2 Corinthians 4:4-6, which has been so foundational for all our thinking in this book. Four verses earlier, Paul builds his teaching of Christ-likeness on the conviction that the gospel reveals "the glory of Christ, who is the image of God" (4:4).

He says in 3:18, "And we all, with unveiled face, *beholding the glory of the Lord*, are being transformed into the same image from one degree of glory to another. For this comes from the Lord who is the Spirit." Notice three things.

1) The pathway to Christ-likeness is "beholding the glory of the Lord." Beholding is becoming. We are transformed "into the . . . image" of the Lord by means of fixing our attention on his glory. In view of all that we have seen in the verses that follow in 2 Corinthians 4:4-6, there is no doubt how we "behold the glory of the Lord" and who the Lord is. The Lord is Christ, and he is the image of God (4:4). Or we can say, the Lord is God seen in the face of Christ (4:6). And the way we "behold the glory of the Lord" is in "the gospel of the glory of Christ." We do not pray for a trance. We pray for grace to meditate on the fullness of the gospel of Christ crucified and risen.

How does this transformation into Christ's image come? At the end of verse 18 Paul says it "comes from the Lord who is the Spirit." This describes, in different words, what we have already seen in 2 Corinthians 4:6. God has "shone in our hearts to give the light of the knowledge of the glory of God in the face of Jesus Christ." This is the way the Holy Spirit does his ongoing change in us. He does not change us directly; he changes us by enabling us to see the glory of Christ.

THE SPIRIT FLIES IN FORMATION BEHIND THE CHRIST-EXALTING GOSPEL

This is crucial to understand. It shows how Christ-exalting the Holy Spirit is. He will not do his sanctifying work by the use of his direct divine power. He will only do it by making the glory of Christ the immediate cause of it. This is the way he works in evangelism, and this is the way he works in sanctification.

In evangelism the Holy Spirit opens the eyes of sinners to see the glory of Christ who is faithfully preached in the gospel. If Christ is not preached and his glory is not exalted, the Holy Spirit does not open our eyes, for there is no glorious Christ displayed for us to see. The Holy Spirit does not do his work apart from the gospel because his work is to open our eyes to see Christ displayed in the gospel, and until the gospel is preached Christ is not there to see. The Holy Spirit, we might say, flies in perfect formation behind the jet of the Christ-exalting gospel. He does his miraculous heart-opening work to make Christ seen and savored as he is preached in the gospel.[5] The Spirit was sent to glorify the Son of God (John 16:14), and he will not save anyone apart from drawing their attention to the glory of the Son in the gospel.

So it is with sanctification. We are transformed into Christ's image—that's what sanctification is—by steadfast seeing and savoring[6] of the glory of Christ. This too is from the Lord who is the Spirit. This is the work of the Spirit: to shine the light of truth on the glory of Christ so that we see it for what it really is, namely, infinitely precious. The work of the Holy Spirit in changing us is not to work directly on our bad habits but to make us admire Jesus

---

[5] See Acts 16:14, "One who heard us was a woman named Lydia, from the city of Thyatira, a seller of purple goods, who was a worshiper of God. *The Lord opened her heart to pay attention to what was said by Paul.*" This is the work of "the Lord who is the Spirit" (2 Cor. 3:18)—to rivet the spiritual attention on what is preached, Jesus Christ.

[6] I include "savoring" with "seeing," even though only seeing (beholding) is explicitly mentioned in 2 Corinthians 3:18, because the seeing cannot be indifferent or displeased—for two reasons: 1) that is not the kind of seeing the Holy Spirit produces, but the kind of seeing we have for Christ before the Spirit works; but here it is the Spirit who is producing the seeing; 2) seeing that is not savoring does not change us into the image of Christ, because not to savor Christ would be the opposite of Christ-like. We do not become like the people we see and do not admire.

Christ so much that sinful habits feel foreign and distasteful. My aim here is not to spell this out in detail,[7] but to point it out so that the gospel does its work decisively by revealing the glory of Christ who is the image of God. Therefore, if we neglect the glory of God in Christ as the greatest gift of the gospel, we cripple the sanctifying work of the church.

We Absorb What We Admire

2) The dynamics of personal transformation in 2 Corinthians 3:18 assume that we are changed into what we admire and fix our attention on. "Beholding the glory of the Lord, [we] are being transformed into the same image." We know this is so from experience. Long looking with admiration produces change. From your heroes you pick up mannerisms and phrases and tones of voice and facial expressions and habits and demeanors and convictions and beliefs. The more admirable the hero is and the more intense your admiration is, the more profound will be your transformation. In the case of Jesus, he is infinitely admirable, and our admiration rises to the most absolute worship. Therefore, when we behold him as we should, the change is profound.

Of course, there is more to it than that. The reflexes of imitation are not the whole story of how we change. Part of what we pick up in looking at Jesus in the gospel is a way of viewing the whole world. That worldview informs all our values and deeply shapes our thinking and decision-making. Another part of what we absorb is greater confidence in Jesus' counsel and his promises. This has its own powerful effect on what we fear and desire and choose. Another part of what we take up from beholding the glory of Christ is greater delight in his fellowship and deeper longing to see him in heaven. This has its own liberating effect from the temptations of this world. All these have their own peculiar way of changing us into the likeness of Christ. Therefore, we should not think that

---

[7] I have tried to spell out in detail this battle for transformation and joy in *When I Don't Desire God* (Wheaton, Ill.: Crossway Books, 2004). See especially the chapter titled, "The Fight for Joy Is a Fight to See."

pursuing likeness to Christ has no other components than just looking at Jesus. Looking at Jesus produces holiness along many different paths.[8]

WE ARE CHANGED BY DEGREES

3) The transformation that comes from beholding the glory of Christ in the gospel happens incrementally. "Beholding the glory of the Lord, [we] are being transformed into the same image *from one degree of glory to another.*" Speaking of our transformation in terms of "glory" shows that Christian glorification begins at conversion, not at death or resurrection. In fact, in Paul's mind sanctification is the first phase of glorification.[9]

Therefore, we should think of the Christian life as conforming more and more to the glorious person of Christ. The first and primary meaning of that conformity is spiritual and moral. We see Christ himself as infinitely beautiful in his spiritual and moral perfections, and therefore infinitely valuable. He is the greatest treasure in the universe. And we see him that way and delight to have found the fountain of all pleasure and the treasure chest of holy joy.

And as we behold him we also come to share more and more in Christ's spiritual perception of the Father and the world. More and more we come to see the preciousness of God the way Christ sees the preciousness of God. And we see that the glory of the Father and the glory of the Son are one glory. There is no choosing one over the other. They have become one God in our heart's affection.

And as we behold the glory of Christ in the gospel and savor his purity, we come to see sin as repugnant, and salvation as mag-

---

[8] For example, alongside my book *When I Don't Desire God* (see note 7), which stresses seeing Christ, I would put *The Purifying Power of Living by Faith in Future Grace* (Sisters, Ore.: Multnomah, 1995), which stresses trusting the promises of God as an essential way of conforming our behavior to Christ. These promises are part of the revelation of the glory of Christ, and the glory of Christ is part of why we embrace the promises so confidently.

[9] This is probably why in the golden chain of Romans 8:30 the term *sanctification* is missing: "And those whom he predestined he also called, and those whom he called he also justified, and those whom he justified he also glorified." When Paul jumps directly from justification to glorification he is not passing over sanctification, because in his mind that process is synonymous with the first phase of glorification and begins at conversion.

nificent. We see people no longer, as Paul says, "according to the flesh" (2 Cor. 5:16), but with a love that "bears all things, believes all things, hopes all things, endures all things" (1 Cor. 13:7). We despair of no one, because in spite of human depravity, "with God all things are possible" (Matt. 19:26). And we see culture no longer merely with the eyes of seduction or despair, but with the eyes of hope. The sovereign, living Christ will someday claim this world for himself. Our spirit is wakened and enlivened by beholding the glory of Christ and his passion to make all things serve the glory of his Father.[10]

FROM ONE DEGREE TO ANOTHER WE LOVE LIKE CHRIST

As our spiritual perception of all things changes by keeping Christ in our steady gaze, our conformity to Christ becomes very practical. Our behavior changes. "A new commandment I give to you," Jesus said, "that you love one another: *just as I have loved you*, you also are to love one another. By this all people will know that you are my disciples, if you have love for one another" (John 13:34-35). As we behold the glory of the Lord in the gospel, the glory of his moral perfections more and more become our desire and our experience, especially the glory of his love for his enemies. "Walk in love, as Christ loved us and gave himself up for us, a fragrant offering and sacrifice to God" (Eph. 5:2). "As the Lord has forgiven you, so you also must forgive" (Col. 2:12). "Have this mind among yourselves, which is yours in Christ Jesus. . . . He humbled himself by becoming obedient to the point of death, even death on a cross" (Phil. 2:5, 8). As we fix our mind's attention and our heart's affection on the glory of Christ's love, more and more we become loving.

---

[10] John 17:1, 4 , "He lifted up his eyes to heaven, and said, 'Father, the hour has come; glorify your Son that the Son may glorify you. . . . I glorified you on earth, having accomplished the work that you gave me to do.'" John 12:27-28, "Now is my soul troubled. And what shall I say? 'Father, save me from this hour'? But for this purpose I have come to this hour. Father, glorify your name."

FROM GLORY TO GLORY INWARDLY, NOT OUTWARDLY—YET

This incremental transformation from glory to glory is not true for our physical bodies in this age. Though God does from time to time heal his people from their diseases in this life, and thus gives them a foretaste of the physical glorification that is coming,[11] the experience of all Christians in this life is progressive aging and weakening and failing health and death. Paul is very clear that this is part of godly Christian experience as we "wait . . . for . . . the redemption of our bodies." "Not only the creation, but we ourselves, who have the firstfruits of the Spirit, groan inwardly as we wait eagerly for adoption as sons, the redemption of our bodies" (Rom. 8:23). But Paul is eager to point out that this outward decay is simultaneous with inward renewal from glory to glory as we fix our gaze on the glory of Christ. This becomes painfully and beautifully explicit in 2 Corinthians 4:16-18:

> *So we do not lose heart. Though our outer nature is wasting away, our inner nature is being renewed day by day. For this slight momentary affliction is preparing for us an eternal weight of glory beyond all comparison, as we look not to the things that are seen but to the things that are unseen. For the things that are seen are transient, but the things that are unseen are eternal.*

The parallels between this text and 2 Corinthians 3:18 are instructive. Being "renewed day by day" is part of being "transformed . . . from one degree of glory to another." And looking "to the things that are unseen" includes "beholding the glory of the Lord"—because "the glory of the Lord" in Paul's mind is in the category of "things that are not seen" by the ordinary physical eye.[12] Seeing the

---

[11] This is probably what Hebrews 6:5 is referring to when it says that some "have tasted the goodness of the word of God and *the powers of the age to come.*"

[12] Thus when Paul says in 2 Corinthians 5:7 that "we walk by faith, not by sight," he does not mean that we do not "behold the glory of the Lord." Rather he means that "we look not to the things that are seen but to the things that are unseen" (2 Cor. 4:18).

unseen glory of Christ in the gospel is the key to inner transformation from day to day and from glory to glory.

Nevertheless this inner transformation is the first step in total
transformation, including the transformation of our bodies. "If the
Spirit of him who raised Jesus from the dead dwells in you, he who
raised Christ Jesus from the dead will also give life to your mortal
bodies through his Spirit who dwells in you" (Rom. 8:11). Being
conformed to the image of Christ will, in due time, include conformity to his glorious body: "Our citizenship is in heaven, and from
it we await a Savior, the Lord Jesus Christ, who will *transform our
lowly body to be like his glorious body*" (Phil. 3:20-21). "Just as
we have borne the image of the man of dust, we shall also bear the
image of the man of heaven" (1 Cor. 15:49).

TOTAL SIGHT WILL MEAN TOTAL CHANGE

This final physical glorification is not disconnected from beholding
the glory of the Lord—neither now nor then. Only by beholding the
glory of the Lord are we kept on the path that leads to the glorified
Christ. There is a "holiness without which no one will see the Lord"
(Heb. 12:14). That holiness is our transformation "from one degree
of glory to another," and that happens by keeping our gaze fixed on
the glory of Christ in the gospel. Therefore, our final meeting with
Christ and our final transformation into his glorious image depends
now on beholding the glory of the Lord.

But the connection between beholding the glory of God in
the face of Christ and being finally and physically changed holds
true at the end as well. This is expressed in 1 John 3:2, "Beloved,
we are God's children now, and what we will be has not yet
appeared; but we know that *when he appears* we shall be like
him,[13] *because we shall see him as he is*." The completion of our
becoming will happen at the completion of our beholding. Seeing
him "as he is" implies that the way we see him now is incomplete.

---

[13] The "him" in this context is God the Father. But the whole drift of Paul's thinking in
2 Corinthians 3:18–4:6 is to show that the glory of the Father shines in the face of Christ, and
the glory of Christ is the glory of the Father. So I am not making a distinction here.

"Now we see in a mirror dimly, but then face to face. Now I know in part; then I shall know fully, even as I have been fully known" (1 Cor. 13:12).

No Gospel and No Salvation Where the Glory of God Is Not Shown and Seen

The overwhelming emphasis in these biblical thoughts is on the glory of God shining in the face of Christ through the gospel. This revelation of God's glory in the gospel is the ground and means of our present and future glorification. The intended effect of these texts is to make it impossible for us to think of our conversion and our character and our consummation as happening apart from our seeing the glory of God in the gospel. The purpose of the gospel—both its central events of Good Friday and Easter, as well as their proclamation in the world—is to make the glory of God in Christ the foundation and the means of all salvation and sanctification and glorification. There is no gospel where the glory of God in Christ is not shown. And there is no salvation through the gospel where the glory of God in Christ is not seen.

There is one more text in the New Testament that explicitly connects the gospel with the glory of God. It is one of the most unusual descriptions of God's relation to the gospel in all the Bible. We turn now to this text in the next chapter.

*Law is not made for a righteous man, but for the
lawless and unruly . . . and if there be any other
thing contrary to the sound doctrine; according to
the gospel of the glory of the blessed God.*

I TIMOTHY I:9-II, ASV

7

THE GOSPEL—THE GLORY OF
THE GLADNESS OF GOD

O ne of the most simple and profound descriptions of the gospel in the New Testament occurs in 1 Timothy 1:11. Paul is describing the right use of the Old Testament law as a means of exposing and restraining sin. He lists twelve particular evils, then adds, "and whatever else is contrary to sound doctrine." Then he continues with one more qualifying phrase: ". . . *according to the gospel of the glory of the blessed God*" (1 Tim. 1:11, ASV).[1] William Mounce comments that the words "gospel of the glory" should not be translated "glorious gospel," as most modern versions do. "Rather τῆς δόξης [the glory] is the actual content of that gospel, i.e., 'the gospel which tells of the glory of God.'"[2]

The gospel reveals the glory of God. The argument of this book is that this revelation is precisely what makes the gospel good news,

---

[1] Most versions (NIV, NASB, RSV, ESV, KJV) treat the phrase "of the glory" in "gospel *of the glory* of the blessed God" as an adjective, and translate it like this: "the *glorious* gospel of the blessed God." But this is not necessary because all these versions translate a similar phrase in 2 Corinthians 4:4 as, "the gospel *of the glory* of Christ," not as "the glorious gospel of Christ." I agree with Henry Alford that the versions should follow the same literal principle in 1 Timothy 1:11 that they followed in 2 Corinthians 4:4. "All propriety and beauty of expression is here [in 1 Timothy 1:11], as always, destroyed by this adjectival rendering. The gospel is 'the glad tidings of the glory of God,' as of Christ in 2 Corinthians 4:4, inasmuch as it reveals to us God in all His glory." Henry Alford, *The Greek Testament*, vol. 3 (Chicago: Moody Press, 1958), 307. Similarly J. N. D Kelly writes, "The gospel tells of the glory of the blessed God (this translation is preferable to 'the glorious gospel' . . .) because, in contrast to the law, which only serves to bring to light the sinfulness of men, it reveals in the person of Christ the divine power, majesty, and compassion." *A Commentary on the Pastoral Epistles* (London: Adam and Charles Black, 1963), 51.
[2] William Mounce, *Pastoral Epistles* (Nashville: Thomas Nelson, 2000), 43.

and that it is not good news if the glory of God is not seen in it. In other words, the glory of God is not marginal or dispensable but is essential to making the good news good.

GOD'S HAPPINESS IS A GREAT PART OF HIS GLORY

In 1 Timothy 1:11 Paul focuses on the gospel as "the glory of the *blessed* God." The word translated "blessed" in this phrase (μακαρίου) is the same one used in the beatitudes of Jesus in Matthew 5:3-11. "Blessed are the poor in spirit, for theirs is the kingdom of heaven. Blessed are those who mourn, for they shall be comforted. Blessed are the meek, for they shall inherit the earth." And so on. The word means "happy" or "fortunate." Paul himself uses it in other places to refer to the happiness of the person whose sins are forgiven (Rom. 4:7) or the person whose conscience is clear (Rom. 14:22). It is astonishing that only here and in 1 Timothy 6:15[3] in the entire Old Testament and New Testament does the word refer to God. Paul has clearly done something unusual, calling God *makarios*, happy.[4]

We may learn from the phrase "the glory of the happy God" that a great part of God's glory is his happiness.[5] It was inconceivable to the apostle Paul that God could be denied infinite joy and still be all-glorious. To be infinitely glorious was to be infinitely happy. He used the phrase, "the glory of the happy God," because it is a glorious thing for God to be as happy as he is. God's glory consists much in the fact that he is happy beyond all our imagination.

NO GOSPEL WITHOUT A GLAD GOD

Even more remarkably, Paul says that this is part of the gospel—"the *gospel* of the glory of the happy God." An essential part of what makes the gospel of the death and resurrection of Christ *good* news

---

[3] 1 Timothy 6:15 says, "He who is the *blessed* [μακάριος] and only Sovereign, the King of kings and Lord of lords."

[4] All the places where God is called "blessed" in the rest of the Greek Bible use another word for "blessed"—*eulogetos*, not *makarios*. "Blessed be the Lord" is εὐλογητός. κύριος (Ps. 41:13 = Ps. 40:4 LXX), but "blessed is the man" is μακάριος ἀνήρ (Ps. 1:1).

[5] For a more extended treatment of God's happiness see John Piper, *The Pleasures of God* (Sisters, Ore.: Multnomah, 2000). At this point I am drawing on things I have said there.

is that the God it reveals is infinitely joyful. No one would want to spend eternity with an unhappy God. If God were unhappy, then the goal of the gospel would not be a happy goal, and that means it would be no gospel at all. But in fact Jesus invites us to spend eternity with a supremely joyful God when he says to us—what he will say at the end of the age—"Enter into the joy of your master" (Matt. 25:23). Jesus lived and died that his joy—God's joy—might be in us and our joy might be full (John 15:11; 17:13). Therefore the gospel is "the gospel of the glory of the happy God."

WHAT'S GOOD ABOUT HAVING A GLAD GOD IN THE GOSPEL?

I must be careful here lest I start writing the book I have already written, *The Pleasures of God: Meditations on God's Delight in Being God.* But at least one of its ideas needs to be here. One of the grounds of God's joy is so crucial for grasping what is supremely good about the gospel that I must explain it here.

The happiness of God is first and foremost a happiness in his Son.[6] Thus when we share in the happiness of God, we share in the very pleasure that the Father has in the Son. Ultimately this is what makes the gospel good news. It opens the way for us to see and savor the glory of Christ. And when we reach that ultimate goal we will find ourselves savoring the Son with the very happiness that the Father has in the Son.

This is why Jesus made the Father known to us. At the end of his great prayer in John 17:26 he said to his Father, "I made known to them your name, and I will continue to make it known, that the love with which you have loved me may be in them, and I in them." The love God has for the Son will be in us. That is, the love for the Son that will be in us will be the Father's love for the Son. We will not merely love the Son with our paltry ability to love. But our love for the Son will be infused with the divine love between the Father and

---

[6] See the chapter "The Pleasure of God in His Son" for the fuller defense and explanation of this truth. Ibid., 25-46.

the Son. Therefore, we should realize from John 17:26 that Jesus made God known so that God's pleasure in his Son might be in us and become our pleasure in Christ.

Imagine being able to enjoy what is infinitely enjoyable with unbounded energy and passion forever. This is not our experience now. Three things stand in the way of our complete satisfaction in this world. One is that nothing here has a personal worth great enough to meet the deepest longings of our hearts. Another is that we lack the strength to savor the best treasures to their maximum worth. And the third obstacle to complete satisfaction is that our joys here come to an end. Nothing lasts.

But if the aim of the gospel—the aim of Jesus in John 17:26 and the aim of Paul in 1 Timothy 1:11 and 2 Corinthians 4:4-6—comes true, all this will change. If God's pleasure in the Son becomes our pleasure, then the object of our pleasure, Jesus, will be inexhaustible in personal worth. He will never become boring or disappointing or frustrating. No greater treasure can be conceived than the very Son of God. Moreover, our ability to savor this inexhaustible treasure will not be limited by human weaknesses. We will enjoy the Son of God with the very enjoyment of his omnipotently happy Father. God's delight in his Son will be in us, and it will be ours. And this will never end, because neither the Father nor the Son ever ends. Their love for each other will be our love for them, and therefore our loving them will never die.

This is the ultimate reason why the gospel is good news. If this does not come true for Christ's people, there is no good news. Therefore, preaching the good news must endeavor to lead people to this. We must make plain to people that if their hope stops short of seeing and savoring the glory of God in Christ, they are not fixing their hearts on the main thing and the best thing Christ died to accomplish—seeing and savoring the glory of God in the face of Christ with everlasting and ever-increasing joy.

*Godly grief produces a repentance that leads to
salvation without regret, whereas
worldly grief produces death.*

2 CORINTHIANS 7:10

*Though it be a deep sorrow for sin that God re-
quires as necessary to salvation,
yet the very nature of it necessarily implies delight.
Repentance of sin is a sorrow arising from
the sight of God's excellency and mercy,
but the apprehension of excellency or mercy
must necessarily and unavoidably beget pleasure
in the mind of the beholder. . . . How much
soever of a paradox it may seem,
it is true that repentance is a sweet sorrow,
so that the more of this sorrow, the more pleasure.*

JONATHAN EDWARDS

8

The Gospel—The Glory of Christ as the Ground of Christ-Exalting Contrition

Gospel-Awakened Contrition as an Echo of Christ's Glory

One surprising way to see that God is the gospel is by penetrating into the soul of gospel-awakened contrition. Those who have dealt deeply with their own sin in relation to the gospel know the paradox that the good news of forgiveness awakens the pain of remorse as well as the joy of release. Only an artificial joy does not pass through sorrow for sin on its way to the thrill of being forgiven.

One of the reasons that many Christians seem to have no thrill at being forgiven through the gospel is that they have not been brokenhearted over their sin. They have not despaired. They have not wrestled with warranted self-loathing. They have not grieved over their sin because of its moral repugnance, but have grieved only because of guilt feelings and threats of hell. The question for us in this chapter is, how does gospel-awakened contrition display the truth that seeing and savoring the glory of Christ is the ultimate and all-important good of the gospel?

JONATHAN EDWARDS HELPS ME AGAIN

Here again I have gotten great help from Jonathan Edwards. The greatest lesson I learned from Edwards is that God is shown to be most beautiful and valuable when his people see him clearly in the gospel and delight in him above all else. In other words, God is most glorified in us when we are most satisfied in him.[1] Which means that you never have to choose between your greatest joy and God's greatest glory.

The question here is: How does this relate to the necessary sorrows of the Christian life, especially the sorrow of gospel-awakened contrition? How does the gospel of the glory of God in the face of Christ (2 Cor. 4:6) relate to the sorrow of contrition? Or to make the question even more pointed, how does the savoring of the glory of God in the gospel relate to the sorrow of gospel-awakened remorse for sin? If the great good of the gospel is savoring the glory of God in the gospel, how can it also produce sorrow? By asking this question we put our previous conclusions to the test. If we are on the right track about God and the gospel, the result should be confirmation.

---

[1] The section in Edwards's writings that made this most clear was:

> God glorifies Himself toward the creatures . . . in two ways: 1. By appearing to . . . their understanding. 2. In communicating Himself to their hearts, and in their rejoicing and delighting in, and enjoying, the manifestations which He makes of Himself. . . . *God is glorified not only by His glory's being seen, but by its being rejoiced in.* When those that see it delight in it, God is more glorified than if they only see it. His glory is then received by the whole soul, both by the understanding and by the heart. God made the world that He might communicate, and the creature receive, His glory; and that it might [be] received both by the mind and heart. He that testifies his idea of God's glory [doesn't] glorify God so much as he that testifies also his approbation of it and his delight in it. Jonathan Edwards, *The "Miscellanies,"* in *The Works of Jonathan Edwards*, vol. 13, ed. Thomas Schafer (New Haven, Conn.: Yale University Press, 1994), 495. Miscellany #448; see also #87 (pp. 251-252); #332 (p. 410); #679 (not in the New Haven volume). Emphasis added.

> See also the comments of Benjamin Warfield on the first question of the Westminster Catechism. The answer, "Man's chief end is to glorify God and to enjoy Him forever" is followed by this comment: "Not to enjoy God, certainly, without glorifying Him, for how can He to whom glory inherently belongs be enjoyed without being glorified? But just as certainly not to glorify God without enjoying Him—for how can He whose glory is His perfections be glorified if He be not also enjoyed?" Benjamin Warfield, "The First Question of the Westminster Shorter Catechism," in *The Westminster Assembly and Its Work*, in *The Works of Benjamin Warfield*, vol. 6 (Grand Rapids, Mich.: Baker, 2003), 400.

SORROW RISES FROM THE SIGHT OF
ALL-SATISFYING GLORY

In a sermon from 1723, titled "The Pleasantness of Religion,"[2] Edwards addressed the question: How does the centrality of savoring the glory of God in the gospel relate to the pain of gospel-awakened contrition? Here is the key insight:

> There is repentance of sin: though it be a deep sorrow for sin that God requires as necessary to salvation, yet the very nature of it necessarily implies delight. *Repentance of sin is a sorrow arising from the sight of God's excellency and mercy*, but the apprehension of excellency or mercy must necessarily and unavoidably beget pleasure in the mind of the beholder. 'Tis impossible that anyone should see anything that appears to him excellent and not behold it with pleasure, and it's impossible to be affected with the mercy and love of God, and his willingness to be merciful to us and love us, and not be affected with pleasure at the thoughts of [it]; but this is the very affection that begets true repentance. How much soever of a paradox it may seem, it is true that repentance is a sweet sorrow, so that the more of this sorrow, the more pleasure.[3]

This is astonishing and true. What he is saying is that to bring people to the sorrow of repentance and contrition, you must bring them first to see the glory of God as their treasure and their delight. This is what happens in the gospel. The gospel is the revelation of "the glory of Christ, who is the image of God" (2 Cor. 4:4). True sorrow over sin is shown by the gospel to be what it really is—the result of failing to savor "the glory of God in the face of Jesus Christ" (2 Cor. 4:6). The sorrow of true contrition is sorrow for not having God as our all-satisfying treasure. But to be sorrowful over not savor-

---

[2] Jonathan Edwards, "The Pleasantness of Religion," in *The Sermons of Jonathan Edwards: A Reader* (New Haven, Conn.: Yale University Press, 1999), 15. His thesis in this sermon is: "It would be worth the while to be religious, if it were only for the pleasantness of it," based on Proverbs 24:13-14.

[3] Ibid., 18-19. Emphasis added. Edwards says similarly in another place, "The same taste which relishes the sweetness of true moral good, tastes the bitterness of moral evil." *Religious Affections*, in *The Works of Jonathan Edwards*, vol. 2, ed. John Smith (New Haven, Conn.: Yale University Press, 1959), 301.

When in a rut, don't focus on yours sins how bad it is. Focus on God— how good He is!

108   GOD IS THE GOSPEL

ing God, we must see God as our treasure, our sweetness. To grieve over not delighting in God, he must have become a delight to us.

THE SEEDS OF DELIGHT BEAR THE FRUIT OF SORROW

How did this happen? How did God become our all-satisfying treasure? It happened through the gospel. The gospel revealed the glory of God in Christ. We saw it. We were awakened to his beauty and worth. The seeds of delight were sown, and the fruit they produced was sorrow—sorrow that for so long we had never savored his glory. Paradoxically this means that true repentance and contrition based on the gospel is preceded by the awakening of a delight in God. To weep savingly over not possessing God as your treasure, he must have become precious to you. The gospel awakens sorrow for sin by awakening a savor for God.

HOW DAVID BRAINERD BROKE THE HEARTS OF INDIANS AND MADE THEM GLAD

Twenty-six years after he preached the sermon on "The Pleasantness of Religion," Jonathan Edwards published the journals of David Brainerd, the young missionary to the American Indians who died in 1747 at the age of twenty-nine. He took this opportunity to illustrate from real life what he had taught about the relationship between the glory of the gospel and the sorrow of contrition.

On August 9, 1745 Brainerd preached to the Indians of Crossweeksung, New Jersey and made this observation:

> There were many tears among them while I was discoursing publicly. . . . Some were much affected with a few words spoken to them in a powerful manner, which caused the persons to cry out in anguish of soul, *although I spoke not a word of terror, but on the contrary, set before them the fullness and all-sufficiency of Christ's merits*, and his willingness to save all that come to him; and thereupon pressed them to come without delay.[4]

---

[4] Jonathan Edwards, *The Life of David Brainerd*, in *The Works of Jonathan Edwards*, vol. 7, ed. Norman Pettit (New Haven, Conn.: Yale University Press, 1985), 310. Emphasis added.

Again on November 30 that same year he preached on Luke 16:19-26 concerning the rich man and Lazarus.

> The Word made powerful impressions upon many in the assembly, especially while I discoursed of the blessedness of Lazarus "in Abraham's bosom" [Luke 16:22]. This, I could perceive, affected them much more than what I spoke of the rich man's misery and torments. And thus it has been usually with them. . . . *They have almost always appeared much more affected with the comfortable than the dreadful truths of God's Word.* And that which has distressed many of them under convictions, is that they found they wanted [=lacked], and could not obtain, *the happiness of the godly.*[5]

This is exactly what Edwards had been preaching twenty-two years earlier. It seems very strange at first. One must taste the happiness of seeing and savoring God in the gospel before one can be truly sorrowful for not having more of that happiness. There is no contradiction between the necessity of sorrow for sin and the necessity of seeing and savoring the glory of God in the gospel. The sweetness of seeing God in the gospel is a prerequisite for godly sorrow for so long scorning that sweetness.

ONLY JOY-BASED SORROW HONORS GOD

The implication of this truth for preaching the gospel is that God himself must be shown as the ultimate good news of the gospel. If people are not awakened to the preciousness of God and the beauty of his glory in the face of Christ, the sorrow of their contrition will not be owing to their failure to cherish God and prize his glory. It will be owing to the fear of hell, or the foolishness of their former behavior, or the waste of their lives. But none of these grounds for contrition, by themselves, is an honor to God.

---

[5] Ibid., 342. Emphasis added.

What Is Disinterested Love?
Pleasure in God Himself

Someone who knows a bit about Jonathan Edwards might raise an objection here. He might say, "Your way of talking about the gospel does not seem faithful to the way Edwards talked. You talk about cherishing and savoring and prizing God in the gospel. These words seem to suggest a strong desire to find pleasure or happiness in God. But Edwards spoke about a 'disinterested' love to God. Are you really being faithful to Edwards and to the apostle Paul by the way you speak of responding to the gospel?"

In response to this good question I would say, it's true that Edwards used the term "disinterested love" in reference to God.

> I must leave it to everyone to judge for himself . . . concerning mankind, how little there is of this disinterested love to God, this pure divine affection, in the world.[6]

> There is no other love so much above a selfish principle as Christian love is, there is no love that is so free and disinterested. God is loved for himself and for his own sake.[7]

But the key to understanding his meaning is found in this last quote. Disinterested love to God is loving God "for himself and for his own sake." In other words, Edwards used the term "disinterested love" to designate love that delights in God for his own greatness and beauty, and to distinguish it from love that delights only in God's gifts. Disinterested love is not love without pleasure. It is love whose pleasure is in God himself.

Disinterested Sweet Entertainment

In fact, Edwards would say that there is no love to God that does not include delight in God. And so if there is a disinterested love to

[6] Jonathan Edwards, *Original Sin*, in *The Works of Jonathan Edwards*, vol. 3, ed. Clyde A. Holbrook (New Haven, Conn.: Yale University Press, 1970), 144.
[7] Jonathan Edwards, *Charity and Its Fruits*, in *Ethical Writings*, in *The Works of Jonathan Edwards*, vol. 8, ed. Paul Ramsey (New Haven, Conn.: Yale University Press, 1989), 264.

Paris Reedhead

God, there is disinterested delight in God. And that is exactly the way he thinks. For example, he says:

> As it is with the love of the saints, so it is with their joy, and spiritual delight and pleasure: the first foundation of it, is not any consideration or conception of their *interest in* divine things; but it primarily consists in the *sweet entertainment* their minds have in the view . . . of the divine and holy beauty of these things, as they are in themselves.[8]

In other words, he says that their "spiritual delight" does not have its foundation in "their *interest* in divine things." That means: their delight in God is not grounded in the gifts he gives them other than himself. That's what "interest" means. Hence their delight in God is "disinterested." Nevertheless, it consists in the "sweet entertainment" of their minds. Thus "disinterested" love for God is the "sweet entertainment" or the joy of knowing God himself.[9] That is what the gospel offers when it reveals "the light of the gospel of the glory of Christ, who is the image of God" (2 Cor. 4:4). That is what must paradoxically precede and produce the sorrow of Christ-exalting contrition.

ANTI-TRIUMPHALISM: SORROWFUL YET ALWAYS REJOICING

One of the reasons for dealing in this chapter with the nature and foundation of Christian contrition is that it enables me to caution against triumphalism. I am aware that when I use the language of prizing and treasuring and delighting and cherishing and being satisfied by the glory of God in the face of Christ, it could sound to some as if all brokenness and suffering and pain and sorrow have

---

[8] Edwards, *Religious Affections*, 249. Emphasis added.
[9] Norman Fiering is right in the following quote if you take "disinterested" in the absolute sense of no benefit whatever, not even the "sweet entertainment" of beholding God. "Disinterested love to God is impossible because the desire for happiness is intrinsic to all willing or loving whatsoever, and God is the necessary end of the search for happiness. Logically one cannot be disinterested about the source or basis of all interest." *Jonathan Edwards's Moral Thought in Its British Context* (Chapel Hill, N.C.: University of North Carolina Press, 1981), 161.

been left behind. That is not true. The Christian never gets beyond the battle with indwelling sin.[10] Life is not all joy above sorrow; life is a battle for joy in the midst of sorrow.[11] The banner that flies over my life and over this book is Paul's paradoxical maxim in 2 Corinthians 6:10, "as sorrowful, yet always rejoicing."

Jonathan Edwards saw the glory of God in the gospel more clearly than most of us and experienced being enthralled with God's fellowship through the gospel.[12] But he also left us one of the most beautiful descriptions of what the glory of God in the gospel produces in the life of the believer. He showed that the God-enthralled vision of Christ in the gospel does not make a person presumptuous—it makes him meek. It produces brokenhearted joy.

> All gracious affections that are a sweet odor to Christ, and that fill the soul of a Christian with a heavenly sweetness and fragrancy, are brokenhearted affections. A truly Christian love, either to God or men, is a humble brokenhearted love. The desires of the saints, however earnest, are humble desires: their hope is a humble hope; and their joy, even when it is unspeakable, and full of glory, is a humble brokenhearted joy, and leaves the Christian more poor in spirit, and more like a little child, and more disposed to a universal lowliness of behavior.[13]

---

[10] Especially helpful on this crucial point is John Owen, *The Works of John Owen*, vol. 6, ed. William Goold (Edinburgh: Banner of Truth, 1967). This volume contains three important works on the battle with remaining sin in believers: *Of the Mortification of Sin in Believers*; *Of Temptation: The Nature and Power of It*; and *The Nature, Power, Deceit, and Prevalency of the Remainders of Indwelling Sin in Believers*. Crossway Books is publishing a new edition of these three works in one volume, due out in 2006, edited by Justin Taylor.

[11] This is why I used the subtitle *How to Fight for Joy* for my book *When I Don't Desire God* (Wheaton, Ill.: Crossway Books, 2004).

[12] "Once as I rode out into the woods for my health in 1737, having alighted from my horse in a retired place, as my manner commonly has been, to walk for divine contemplation and prayer, I had a view, that for me was extraordinary, of the glory of the Son of God, as Mediator between God and man, and his wonderful, great, full, pure and sweet grace and love and meek, gentle condescension . . . which continued, as near as I can judge, about an hour; which kept me the greater part of the time in a flood of tears, and weeping aloud." This is taken from Edwards's "Personal Narrative," in *Jonathan Edwards: Representative Selections*, ed. Clarence H. Faust and Thomas H. Johnson (New York: Hill and Wang, 1935), 69.

[13] Jonathan Edwards, *Religious Affections*, 348-349.

LEAVING SATAN ALIVE: THE PRICE OF SHOWING CHRIST PRECIOUS

In fact, God is so intentional about revealing the glory of the cruci-fied Christ in the gospel, and producing Christians who are con-formed to Christ's self-emptying love (2 Cor. 3:18), that not only does he make the cross the central revelation of his glory in this age, but he also leaves Satan in the world to magnify the power and wisdom and beauty of meekness.

Have you ever wondered why God does not simply snuff Satan and his demons out of existence now?[14] It is strange that God, with total sovereign rights over Satan, his archenemy, would allow him to do so much harm. God has the right and power to throw him into the lake of fire. God will one day do away with Satan altogether (Rev. 20:3, 10). That will be no injustice to Satan. Nor would it be unjust for God to do it today. So why doesn't he, in view of how much misery Satan causes?

Is it because there is a chance the devil and his angels will repent? No. They are irredeemable. Jesus said that "eternal fire [has been] prepared for the devil and his angels" (Matt. 25:41). Jesus' brother Jude wrote that the fallen angels are being "kept in eternal chains under gloomy darkness until the judgment of the great day" (Jude 6).

Why then does God tolerate Satan? We find the key in remem-bering that Satan hates the gospel. "The god of this world [Satan] has blinded the minds of the unbelievers, to keep them from seeing the light of the gospel of the glory of Christ" (2 Cor. 4:4). This is a clue to why God gives Satan so much leash. God's aim is to magnify the glory of Christ through the gospel.

In other words, God's purpose is to defeat Satan in a way that glorifies not only Christ's raw power, but also his superior beauty and worth and desirability. Christ could simply exert sovereign power and snuff Satan out. That would indeed glorify Christ's

---

[14] In the remainder of this chapter I am drawing on, and partially quoting, what I have written in *Life as a Vapor* (Sisters, Ore.: Multnomah, 2004), 77-81.

power. But it would not display so clearly the superior worth of Jesus over Satan. It would not display the transforming beauty and power of Christ's meekness and humility and lowliness and self-emptying love. The aim of the gospel is to put the glory of the crucified Christ on display and to shame Satan by the millions of people who "turn from darkness to light and from the power of Satan to God" (Acts 26:18) and forsake Satan's lies in preference for the beauty of Christ in the gospel.[15]

This way of defeating Satan is more costly than simply snuffing him out. Christ suffered for this triumph, and the world suffers. But God's values are not so easily reckoned. If Christ obliterated all demons now (which he could do), his sheer power would be seen as glorious, but his superior beauty and worth would not shine so brightly as when God's people renounce the promises of Satan, trust in Christ's blood and righteousness, and take pleasure in the greater glory of Jesus revealed in the gospel.

SATAN GIVES WAY WHEN GOD IS THE GOSPEL

This means that the point of this book is stunningly important to God. God aims that his glory be seen and savored in the gospel so clearly that the power of Satan is broken, and it becomes plain to all that the sweetness of the crucified Christ is more powerful than the enticements of Satan. It is not a small thing to fail to display God as the greatest gift of the gospel. It plays into the hands of the devil and contradicts God's design to break Satan's power by the revelation of the superior beauty of Christ in the gospel.

So let us preach and live the gospel so as to display Christ. Let us take up arms and defeat the devil by being bold and glad in the superior glory of the Son of God! I do not say it is easy. It is very costly. The path of love that leads from the cross of Christ to the glory of Christ is a road of sacrifice. Christ's superior beauty over

---

[15] And if Satan sneers that he still has millions whom he has persuaded to stay in his darkness, this will only serve to magnify the justice of God in condemnation and the mercy of God for those who escape. God knows the proportion of things and how best to make much of all the attributes of Christ.

Satan and sin is seen best when we are willing to suffer for it. One of the greatest blows against the power of darkness comes from the blood of martyrs. "They have conquered him [Satan!] by the blood of the Lamb and by the word of their testimony, for they loved not their lives even unto death" (Rev. 12:11). This is the kind of life that grows from seeing God as the gospel.

Acts 2:22-24
I do not count
my life as any worth

He predestined us . . . to the praise of the glory
of his grace.

EPHESIANS 1:5-6, NASB

For through him we both have access in
one Spirit to the Father.

EPHESIANS 2:18

He comes on that day to be glorified in his saints,
and to be marveled at among all
who have believed.

2 THESSALONIANS 1:10

And this is eternal life, that they know you
the only true God, and Jesus Christ
whom you have sent.

JOHN 17:3

9

THE GOSPEL—THE GIFT OF GOD HIMSELF OVER AND IN ALL HIS SAVING AND PAINFUL GIFTS

THE LINE BETWEEN GOD-CHERISHING GRATITUDE AND GIFT-CHERISHING IDOLATRY

The question I ask in this chapter and the next is: How do all the gifts that flow to us from the gospel relate to God as the ultimate and all-important gift of the gospel? The challenge of these two chapters is to walk a fine line between belittling the gifts of God and making the gifts of God into god. It's the line between God-cherishing gratitude and gift-cherishing idolatry. The truth I will try to unfold is that all the gifts of God are given for the sake of revealing more of God's glory, so that the proper use of them is to rest our affections not on them but through them on God alone.

What I mean by resting our affections is that the desires of our hearts find their end point—their goal, their resting place—only in God, even though, as it were, they ride up to God on a thousand gifts. Augustine said, "Thou madest us for Thyself, and our heart is restless, until it repose in Thee."[1] This restlessness is a good thing when we find ourselves delighting in one of God's gifts. Gifts of

---

[1] St. Augustine, *The Confessions of St. Augustine* (New York: Washington Square Press, 1962), 1.

God *should* be enjoyed, whether the gift is salvation (1 Pet. 1:4-5) or food (1 Tim. 4:3; 6:17). But if our affections rest there, we become idolaters. So the aim of this chapter and the next is to show from Scripture how blood-bought gifts—one could say, gifts of the gospel—point away from themselves to the one great gift of the gospel, God himself.

THE GOSPEL GIFT OF PREDESTINATION

Consider first God's manifold gifts that come to us in the accomplishment of our salvation. How shall we rejoice in them? *Predestination* is one of the first gifts of the gospel, even though it preceded the death of Christ in eternity. The spotless lamb, Jesus Christ, who was slain for our sins, was foreknown before the foundation of the world (1 Pet. 1:20). Because of this, God gave us grace in Christ before the ages began (2 Tim. 1:9). Therefore, Paul says, "God predestined us for adoption *through Jesus Christ*" (Eph. 1:5). This predestination was God's purpose to adopt us and make us holy and blameless before him in love.

How then shall we rejoice in this amazing blood-bought gift of predestination? Paul gives the answer in Ephesians 1:6. "He predestined us . . . *to the praise of the glory of His grace*" (NASB). God's aim in our predestination is that we admire and make much of the glory of his grace. In other words, the aim of predestining us is that grace would be put on display as glorious, and that we would see it and savor it and sing its praises. The glory of grace is the glory of God acting graciously. Therefore the aim of predestination is that we see and savor God in his gracious saving action of predestination. The goal of predestination, and of the gospel acts that purchased it, is that we would be glad in praising the grace of God.

HOW SHALL WE REJOICE IN THE GOSPEL GIFT OF INCARNATION?

In order for God to purchase the gift of predestination, God had to send his Son into the world as a human being to die in our place and

bear the wrath of God and fulfill the righteousness we have failed
to perform. This entrance of the Son of God into the world is called
the *incarnation*. It is a great gift of God that we did not deserve.
Like predestination it was both the result of and the condition for
the atoning death of Christ. It was a result in the sense that God
foresaw what he would do at Calvary in the death of his Son to justify the apparently unjust act of humiliating his Son in thirty-three
years of divine self-emptying. The death of Christ would vindicate
the righteousness of God in sending Christ and exposing him to
finitude and affliction. This blood-bought vindication would make
it possible for God to be both just and the one who justifies sinners
who believe in him (Rom. 3:24-26).

How then shall we rejoice in the gift of the incarnation? Paul
answers in Romans 15:8-9. "Christ became a servant to the circum-
cised [that is, he became incarnate as the Jewish Messiah] to show
God's truthfulness . . . *in order that the Gentiles might glorify God
for his mercy.*" The point here is that Christ's incarnation as the
servant of the Lord was a beautiful display of mercy. That mercy
was a manifestation of the riches of the glory of God. Our response
to that display of glory-revealing mercy is to let our heart ride up
the beam of mercy into the presence of God and there see and savor
the glory of God. The affections of our joy should not rest on the
gift but ride the gift up to God himself.

Paul made the same point in Philippians 2:6-11. If we collapse
these sentences down to the beginning and the ending, we can see
clearly the ultimate reason for the incarnation. It says that Christ
was "born in the likeness of men . . . becoming obedient to the
point of death . . . so that . . . every tongue [would] confess that
Jesus Christ is Lord, to the glory of God the Father." The ultimate
aim of the incarnation was that through Christ people would see
the Lordship of Christ and the glory of God. The whole story of
Christ's incarnate life and death and resurrection was the brightest beam of glory that has ever shone down from the brightness
of God. When this gospel story is rightly proclaimed, that glory is

displayed. If this glory is not shown and seen, the greatest good of the gospel is not seen, and there is no salvation.

RECONCILIATION: THE ARRIVAL OF GOD AND JOY

In Chapter 3 ("The Gospel—'Behold Your God!'") we have already dealt with justification by faith and the forgiveness of sins. We showed that these are gospel gifts aimed at removing obstacles between us and God. They are not good news in and of themselves. They make possible the *reconciliation* between sinners and a holy God. This reconciliation brings us home to God. The focus of reconciliation is that we now may enjoy the presence of God without condemnation.

Therefore, after Paul said in Romans 5:10-11 that "we are *reconciled*," he went on to say, "More than that, we also *rejoice in God* through our Lord Jesus Christ, through whom we have now received reconciliation." The aim of this reconciliation is not safe and sullen solidarity. The aim is that we "rejoice in God through our Lord Jesus Christ." God is the focus of the reconciliation. The joy of reconciliation is joy in God. Therefore when we preach the gospel of reconciliation, the focus must not be merely the removal of enmity, but the arrival of joy in God. Seeing and savoring the reconciled God is the ultimate good in the good news of Jesus Christ.

CHRIST BLED THAT WE MIGHT BE BROUGHT NEAR TO GOD

Whether one thinks of the work of Christ as accomplishing reconciliation or propitiation or penal satisfaction or redemption or justification or forgiveness of sins or liberation, the aim of them all is summed up in the ultimate gift of God himself. First Peter 3:18 is the clearest statement: "Christ also suffered once for sins, the righteous for the unrighteous, *that he might bring us to God*." Ephesians 2:13-18 is the next most explicit statement of this truth. "In Christ Jesus you who once were far off have been *brought near* by the blood of Christ . . . . that he might . . . reconcile us both to

God in one body through the cross. . . . For through him *we both have access in one Spirit to the Father.*" The ultimate aim of the blood of Christ is that we be "brought near" to God and "have access in one Spirit to the Father."

GOD'S BEST GIFT: BEING ETERNALLY ENTHRALLED WITH GOD

This is crucial to see. Many people seem to embrace the good news without embracing God. There is no sure evidence that we have a new heart just because we want to escape hell. That's a perfectly natural desire, not a supernatural one. It doesn't take a new heart to want the psychological relief of forgiveness, or the removal of God's wrath, or the inheritance of God's world. All these things are understandable without any spiritual change. You don't need to be born again to want these things. The devils want them.

It is not wrong to want them. Indeed it is folly not to. But the evidence that we have been changed is that we want these things because they bring us to the enjoyment of God. This is the greatest thing Christ died for. This is the greatest good in the good news. Why is that? Because we were made to experience full and lasting happiness from seeing and savoring the glory of God. If our best joy comes from something less, we are idolaters and God is dishonored. He created us in such a way that his glory is displayed through our joy in it. The gospel of Christ is the good news that at the cost of his Son's life, God has done everything necessary to enthrall us with what will make us eternally and ever-increasingly happy—namely, himself.[2]

THE CONSUMMATION OF THE GOSPEL: MARVELING AT THE MIGHTY CHRIST

The *consummation* of our salvation at the second coming of Christ was secured by the blood of Christ and preached in the gospel. Christ's death and resurrection gave him power over death on behalf

---

[2] The previous two paragraphs are based on Chapter 22, "Christ Suffered and Died to Bring Us to God," in John Piper, *The Passion of Jesus Christ* (Wheaton, Ill.: Crossway Books, 2004), 62-63.

of all who are his. "I died, and behold I am alive forevermore, and I have the keys of Death and Hades" (Rev. 1:18). There is an iron-clad connection between Christ's victory over death and our victory over death. "If the Spirit of him who raised Jesus from the dead dwells in you, he who raised Christ Jesus from the dead will also give life to your mortal bodies" (Rom. 8:11). "God raised the Lord and will also raise us up by his power" (1 Cor. 6:14; cf. 2 Cor. 4:14).

And when Christ comes to raise us from the dead, he "will transform our lowly body to be like his glorious body, by the power that enables him even to subject all things to himself" (Phil. 3:21). The great victory note will be sounded: "'Death is swallowed up in victory.' 'O death, where is your victory? O death, where is your sting?' The sting of death is sin, and the power of sin is the law. But thanks be to God, who gives us the victory through our Lord Jesus Christ" (1 Cor. 15:54-57).

But what will be the focus in this great hour of consummation? Second Thessalonians 1:7-10 gives a clear answer. The focus will be on the glory of Christ, and we will marvel at it.

> *The Lord Jesus [will be] revealed from heaven with his mighty angels in flaming fire, inflicting vengeance on those who do not know God and on those who do not obey the gospel of our Lord Jesus. They will suffer the punishment of eternal destruction, away from the presence of the Lord and from the glory of his might, when he comes on that day to be glorified in his saints, and to be marveled at among all who have believed, because our testimony to you was believed.*

The aim of his coming and the consummation of the gospel promise is that he will "be glorified in his saints" and be "marveled at among all who have believed." This will be our great joy and his great honor. That is the way God planned it to be. We get the joy; he gets the glory. The goal of the consummation of the gospel is the glory of God in the face of Christ. And the highest good in the good news is that we see and savor the One who is infinitely worthy of being glorified and marveled at.

ETERNAL LIFE: EXTENDING AND PERFECTING THE PLEASURES OF KNOWING GOD

Of course, this glorious event is commencement as well as consummation. It is the beginning of *eternal life*. It is true that we have already been given the gift of eternal life through faith in Christ. "Whoever believes in the Son *has* eternal life" (John 3:36). Notice the present tense. We *have*, not just *will* have, eternal life. This is real and precious and permanent. "I give them eternal life, and they will never perish, and no one will snatch them out of my hand" (John 10:28).

But it is also true that the fullness of eternal life begins at the resurrection. Jesus said, "Truly, I say to you, there is no one who has left house or wife or brothers or parents or children, for the sake of the kingdom of God, who will not receive many times more in this time, and *in the age to come eternal life*" (Luke 18:29-30). The fullness of eternal life begins in the age to come. Therefore, Paul says that we have "become heirs according to *the hope of eternal life*" (Titus 3:7). Eternal life is something we are hoping for.

Eternal life is one of the most treasured gifts of the gospel. It is rooted in one of the most familiar and best-loved gospel promises, John 3:16: "For God so loved the world, that he gave his only Son, that whoever believes in him should not perish but have *eternal life*." So the promise of eternal life is connected to the love of God and the gift of his Son. What then is this gift that flows from the gospel and from the love of God?

Jesus tells us in the prayer of John 17. He prays to his Father, "And this is eternal life, that they know you the only true God, and Jesus Christ whom you have sent" (v. 3). In other words, the gift of the gospel called eternal life is not the mere extension of every earthly pleasure. It is the extension and perfection of the pleasures of knowing God and his Son Jesus Christ. "This is eternal life, that they know you the only true God." All other gods must go. All other delights that are not delights in God must go—not because anything good must be taken away, but to make room for what is infinitely best, God himself. Eternal life is a great gift of the gospel.

And it becomes *the* great gift of the gospel when we experience it as knowing and enjoying the only true God and his Son forever.

THE GOSPEL BOUGHT ALL THINGS THAT ARE GOOD FOR US

We might call these gifts the saving gifts of the gospel: predestination, incarnation, justification, reconciliation, consummation, eternal life, etc. But there are others. The gospel has unleashed the omnipotent mercy of God so that thousands of other gifts flow to us from the gospel heart of God. I am thinking of a text like Romans 8:32: "He who did not spare his own Son but gave him up for us all, how will he not also with him graciously give us all things?" This means that the heart of the gospel—God's not sparing his own Son—is the guarantee that "all things" will be given to us.

All things? What does that mean? It means the same thing that Romans 8:28 means: "And we know that for those who love God *all things* work together for good, for those who are called according to his purpose." God takes "all things" and makes them serve our ultimate good. It doesn't mean we get everything our imperfect hearts want. It means we get what's good for us.

THE GOSPEL SECURES THAT EVERY REAL NEED WILL BE MET

Compare this with Philippians 4:19: "My God will supply *every need* of yours according to his riches in glory in Christ Jesus." Every need! Does that mean we never have hard times? Evidently not. Seven verses earlier Paul said, "I know how to be brought low, and I know how to abound. In any and every circumstance, I have learned the secret of facing plenty *and hunger*, abundance *and need*. I can do all things through him who strengthens me" (vv. 12-13). This is amazing. God meets "every need" (v. 19). Therefore, I have learned how to face "hunger" and "need" (v. 12). I can do "all things" through him who strengthens me—including be hungry and be in need! I conclude from this that for Christians everything we need—in order to do God's will and magnify him—will be supplied. According to Romans 8:32 this was secured by the gospel.

It is stated even more strikingly in Romans 8:35-37. Here the love of Christ guarantees that we will be more than conquerors in every circumstance, including the circumstance of being killed. "Who shall separate us from the love of Christ? Shall tribulation, or distress, or persecution, or famine, or nakedness, or danger, or sword? As it is written, 'For your sake we are being killed all the day long; we are regarded as sheep to be slaughtered.' No, in all these things we are more than conquerors through him who loved us." Astonishing! We are more than conquerors as we are being killed all day long! So nothing can separate us from Christ's love, *not* because Christ's love protects us from harm, but because it protects us from the ultimate harm of unbelief and separation from the love of God. The gospel gift of God's love is better than life.

ALL THINGS ARE YOURS, INCLUDING DEATH

"Neither death nor life . . . will be able to separate us from the love of God in Christ Jesus our Lord" (Rom. 8:38-39). In fact, not only can death not separate us from the love of God, it is, along with every other hardship, a gospel gift. Listen to the way Paul says it in 1 Corinthians 3:21-23, "Let no one boast in men. For all things are yours, whether Paul or Apollos or Cephas or the world or life *or death* or the present or the future—all are yours, and you are Christ's, and Christ is God's." All things are yours—including death! Death is included in our treasure chest of gifts from God through the gospel. So in one text Paul says that we are "more than conquerors" in death. And in another text he says that all things are ours, including death. I take him to mean that because of the truths of Romans 8:28 and 8:32 God takes every hardship and makes it serve us, including death. Death is "ours"—our servant. The fact that we are "more than conquerors" means that death doesn't just lie dead at our feet after the battle—it is taken captive and made to serve us.

And how does death serve us? How does the blood-bought

servitude of death bless the children of God? Paul answers, "For to me to live is Christ, and *to die is gain*" (Phil. 1:21). Why is dying gain? He answers two verses later: "My desire is to depart and be with Christ, for that is far better." Being with Christ after death is "far better" than staying on earth. That is why we are more than conquerors when death seems to triumph. It becomes a door to better fellowship with Christ.

HOW JOHN OWEN PREPARED FOR DEATH

When John Owen, the greatest theologian and pastor in England, was dying in 1683 his whole focus was on the glory of Christ. His last book was titled *Meditations on the Glory of Christ*. In his understanding the best way to get ready to die was by meditating on that glory:

> If our future blessedness shall consist in being where He is, and beholding of His glory, what better preparation can there be for it than in a constant previous contemplation of that glory in the revelation that is made in the Gospel, unto this very end that by a view of it we may be gradually transformed into the same glory.[3]

William Payne, the editor of Owen's book on the glory of Christ, visited him near the end and records that Owen said to him, "O, brother Payne, the long-wished for day is come at last, in which I shall see the glory in another manner than I have ever done or was capable of doing in this world."[4]

This is what Paul meant when he said that being with Christ was "far better." We will see the glory of Christ "in another manner." A vastly greater manner. This is why God called us to himself in the first place: "God is faithful, by whom you were called into the fellowship of his Son, Jesus Christ our Lord" (1 Cor. 1:9). The apostle Paul and John Owen were persuaded that death was not an

---

[3] John Owen, *Meditations and Discourses on the Glory of Christ in His Person, Office, and Grace*, in *The Works of John Owen*, vol. 1 (Edinburgh: Banner of Truth, 1965), 275.
[4] Peter Toon, *God's Statesman: The Life and Work of John Owen* (1971; reprint, Eugene, Ore.: Wipf & Stock, 2005), 171.

interruption of that fellowship, but a deepening of it. So Paul said, "We would rather be away from the body and at home with the Lord" (2 Cor. 5:8).

MORE PAINFUL AND PURIFYING GIFTS OF THE GOSPEL

This is all very strange. Because of the gospel, God promises to "give us all things" with Christ (Rom. 8:32). The "all things" turns out to include not just pleasant things but terrible things like tribulation, distress, persecution, famine, nakedness, danger, sword, and death. These are all gospel gifts purchased for us by the blood of Christ. Death is a gift because it takes us more quickly to the great good of the gospel—seeing and savoring the glory of God in the face of Christ.

What about these other gifts—tribulation, distress, and so on? How are they benefits that are bought by the gospel? How are they part of the "all things" in Romans 8:32 and 28 and Philippians 4:13? The answer is that in the merciful sovereignty of Christ, empowered by his own blood, these sufferings accomplish the greatest good of the gospel, a more pure and authentic and deeply satisfying seeing and savoring of God in Christ.

THE GOSPEL DESIGN OF PAUL'S SUFFERING— AND OURS

Paul shows us this in several places. For example, in 2 Corinthians 1:8-9 he describes God's gospel design in his terrible sufferings in Asia: "We do not want you to be ignorant, brothers, of the affliction we experienced in Asia. For we were so utterly burdened beyond our strength that we despaired of life itself. Indeed, we felt that we had received the sentence of death. But *that was to make us rely not on ourselves but on God who raises the dead.*" This is not the design of the devil. It is the design of God. Paul's life-threatening suffering was designed by God to keep him close to God. The aim of the gospel is not an easy life. It is deeper knowledge of God and deeper trust in God.

Similarly in 2 Corinthians 12:7-10 Paul explains how Christ refused to take away his suffering because of a better purpose than pain-free existence.

> *To keep me from being too elated by the surpassing greatness of the revelations, a thorn was given me in the flesh, a messenger of Satan to harass me, to keep me from being too elated. Three times I pleaded with the Lord about this, that it should leave me. But he said to me, "My grace is sufficient for you, for my power is made perfect in weakness." Therefore I will boast all the more gladly of my weaknesses, so that the power of Christ may rest upon me. For the sake of Christ, then, I am content with weaknesses, insults, hardships, persecutions, and calamities. For when I am weak, then I am strong.*

This thorny "messenger of Satan" was designed by God for sanctifying, gospel purposes well beyond the reach of Satan. Satan becomes the lackey of the risen Christ. What was Christ's purpose in Paul's suffering? "My power is made perfect in weakness." Now this is unintelligible to those who define love as helping us get out of pain quickly. It is also unintelligible to those who say that Christ cannot be loving if he is letting Paul suffer to magnify his own glory. But that is exactly what he is doing. This is why the love of God in the gospel looks so foolish to people. How can this be love?

Paul evidently thinks it is, because his response is utterly contrary to ordinary thinking. He says, "Therefore"—that is, because Christ is magnified in my weakness—"I will boast *all the more gladly* of my weaknesses, so that the power of Christ may rest upon me." "All the more gladly"? This is a strange man. No. Rather we should say, the gospel is strange. Its goal is not my immediate ease. Its goal is my being so in love with Christ and so passionate about his glory that when my suffering can highlight his worth I will bear it "gladly."

God did not spare his own Son. Therefore all things are yours— "the world or life or death (or thorns in the flesh or life-threatening persecution) all are yours, and you are Christ's, and Christ is God's." These are gospel gifts because by the blood of Christ they help bring about the goal of the gospel. This goal is not our ease or wealth or safety in this age, but our dependence on Christ and our delight in his glory.

FAITH TASTES WHAT IS CHRIST-EXALTING AND EMBRACES IT

What is the relationship between the gospel goal of depending on Christ and delighting in his glory? We saw that the design of God in Paul's suffering in Asia (and ours) was "to make us *rely* not on ourselves but *on God* who raises the dead" (2 Cor. 1:9). And we saw that the upshot of Christ's severe mercy in leaving his "thorn in the flesh" was that Paul "gladly" boasted in his weaknesses. In other words, he had found a more compelling pleasure in Christ than in physical comfort. How do reliance and delight relate? How does faith in Christ relate to delight in Christ? How do trusting God and savoring the glory of God relate to each other?

To answer this we should ask: What should faith trust Christ for? It would be defective to trust him to supply pornography. I only use this gross example to make the principle clear. Faith is not saving faith if it tries to trust Christ for the wrong things. So this makes clear that trust per se, without reference to what we trust him for, is *not* the essence of a saving relationship to Christ. Something else must be present in faith if it is to be saving faith that honors Christ rather than just using him. Saving faith must have a quality to it that tastes what is Christ-exalting and embraces it.

HOW DO YOU TRUST THE STATEMENT, "I AM YOUR SOUL'S SATISFACTION"?

We must trust Christ for what he tells us to trust him for, namely, his gifts and promises. And what are they? The best gift purchased and promised by the gospel is the gift of God himself, revealed in Christ and offered to us for our enjoyment. What does it mean to trust a person who says, "Whoever believes in me shall never thirst" (John 6:35)? Or, to put it differently, what does it mean to trust a person who says, "My beauty and my glory are your soul's deep-est satisfaction"? It means that trust must taste and embrace that satisfaction. Trust must experience its thirst being satisfied. To say, "I trust that you are *now* my soul's deepest satisfaction" and yet to have no taste of that satisfaction is a contradiction.

To be sure we must trust Christ for the *fullness* of this satisfaction in the age to come. We do not experience that now. But we have tasted it in some measure. That is what Paul means when he says, "We walk by faith, not by sight" (2 Cor. 5:7). We don't see or savor the fullness of God's glory now. "Now we see in a mirror dimly, but then face to face. Now I know in part; then I shall know fully, even as I have been fully known" (1 Cor. 13:12). But, while the fullness of sight waits for the age to come, there is a spiritual sight now (2 Cor. 4:4, 6; Eph. 1:18), and faith in the spiritual sight of glory now includes savoring the glory now.

That's what it means to trust one who offers himself as our "exceeding joy." "I will go to the altar of God, to *God my exceeding joy*" (Ps. 43:4). So faith has tasted the glory of God in Christ and treasures it enough that the fullness of it is worth waiting for and suffering for. Faith has seen the truth that part of Christ's glory is his trustworthiness. Therefore, faith can cast itself on the promise of Christ and trust that the fullness of glory and the fullness of joy will surely come.

A MILLION GOSPEL MERCIES, BUT NONE GOOD WITHOUT GOD

The point of this chapter and the one to follow is that the gospel has unleashed a million mercies on the people of Christ, but that none of these is good news in and of itself. They are all good to the degree that they make possible the one great good—namely, knowing and enjoying God himself. Therefore, the gospel must be preached and believed and lived as "the light of the knowledge of the glory of God in the face of Jesus Christ" (2 Cor. 4:6). That is what I mean by saying God is the gospel.

Though the fig tree should not blossom,
nor fruit be on the vines,
the produce of the olive fail and the fields yield no food,
the flock be cut off from the fold and there be
no herd in the stalls, yet I will rejoice in the Lord;
I will take joy in the God of my salvation.

HABAKKUK 3:17-18

10

THE GOSPEL—THE GIFT OF GOD HIMSELF OVER AND IN ALL HIS PLEASANT GIFTS

There are a thousand gospel blessings purchased for believers by the blood of Christ. We saw this in Romans 8:32 in the previous chapter. "He who did not spare his own Son but gave him up for us all, how will he not also with him graciously give us *all things*?" We have seen that the "all things" include death and persecution and thorns in the flesh. But "all things" also includes pleasant things. That is what we turn to in this chapter. And the question continues: How do God's good gifts relate to God himself as the greatest gift of the gospel?

ALL ANSWERS TO PRAYER ARE BLOOD-BOUGHT GIFTS OF THE GOSPEL

One of the strongest biblical warnings not to use the God of the gospel just to get his gospel gifts comes in relation to prayer. This was especially relevant to my wife and me as we were wrestling with some hard things in our lives as I was writing this book. We wanted God to do something and were praying with tears and great earnestness. But there came a point where I felt that we were not praying in a way that honored God. So I wrote a note to my wife that expresses part of the biblical warning I just mentioned:

The strong sense I have now as I woke early and could not go back to sleep was that the Lord wants us to trust him. He seemed to admonish me that my pleadings were not faith-filled. I was starting to nag. It is not good to nag God. I was not surrendering and handing the burden over to him. I was treating him the way I have sometimes treated you in pleading for something with the tone that if I don't get it I will be perpetually unhappy. That is unbelief, since it elevates God's gift above God. So I was encouraged by these thoughts to "Cast [my] burden on the *Lord*," and trust the promise that "he will sustain [me]; he will never permit the righteous to be moved." And for our guidance I take Psalm 25:8, "Good and upright is the LORD; therefore he instructs sinners in the way." That is one of the qualifications I confidently bring to my prayers: I am a sinner.

Now how does this experience and the warning of Scripture against using God to get his gifts make plain what the greatest gift of the gospel is? Merciful answers to prayer are blood-bought gifts of the gospel. Hebrews 4:16 teaches us that we can "draw near to the throne of grace" with confidence and "find grace to help in time of need" because "we have a great high priest" (v. 14). The reason Jesus Christ, our High Priest, makes answers to prayer possible is that he is not like the Old Testament priests: "He has no need, like those high priests, to offer sacrifices daily, first for his own sins and then for those of the people, since he did this once for all when he offered up himself" (Heb. 7:27).

This is why all the promises of God are Yes in Christ and why we pray in Jesus' name. "All the promises of God find their Yes in him. That is why it is through him that we utter our Amen to God for his glory" (2 Cor. 1:20). Therefore Jesus said, "I chose you and appointed you that you should go and bear fruit . . . so that whatever you ask the Father *in my name*, he may give it to you" (John 15:16).

Answered prayer is based on Jesus' priestly intercession for us, and that intercession is based on the blood he shed to remove our sins and release the flood of prayer-answering grace. Therefore, all the blessings we receive in answer to prayer, we owe to the gospel of

Christ crucified and risen. They are not automatic blessings. They are blood-bought for sinners like us.

How Prayer Can Make a Cuckold out of God

Now comes the strongest warning in the New Testament against making prayer the place where we use God to get his gifts but not himself. James 4:2-5 sounds the warning:

> *You desire and do not have, so you murder. You covet and cannot obtain, so you fight and quarrel. You do not have, because you do not ask. You ask and do not receive, because you ask wrongly, to spend it on your passions. You adulterous people! [literally: adulteresses!] Do you not know that friendship with the world is enmity with God? Therefore whoever wishes to be a friend of the world makes himself an enemy of God. Or do you suppose it is to no purpose that the Scripture says, "He yearns jealously over the spirit that he has made to dwell in us"?*

Why does he call us "adulteresses" when we pray? It's because we ask God for things to indulge our desires that are not desires for him. This is startling—that in the moment of one of the most pious acts of our religion, prayer, we can be making a cuckold out of God. *Cuckold* is an Old English word for a man whose wife is unfaithful. The picture in this text is that God is our faithful, generous husband. So we go to him and ask for, say, fifty dollars, and he gives it to us. Then we take it and walk away from him and go to the end of the hall where our illicit lover has a room. That's the way God looks at praying that does not make "Hallowed be thy name" the heart-cry of every petition.

When James says at the end of this text that God "yearns jealously over the spirit that he has made to dwell in us," he means: God wants your heart when you pray. God will not be a mere dispenser of gifts for those who have no delight in God himself.

What then do we learn here about the gospel? It was the gospel that purchased and promised all our answers to prayer. What we learn is that the aim of the gospel is not mainly to give us God's gifts, but to give us God. All his gifts are good. But in and through them all, the aim is to see more of God's glory and to savor more of his infinitely beautiful moral perfections displayed in the gospel.

CAN GRATITUDE TO GOD BE IDOLATROUS?

What if someone said, "Maybe the problem with the wife who asked for $50 from her husband is that she isn't really thankful. Maybe our problem in dealing with God and the gospel is that we are not grateful." Well, that is certainly part of our problem. But it is not our main problem. That diagnosis does not go to the root of the problem because it is possible to feel truly thankful to someone for a gift and not love the giver.

Jonathan Edwards saw to the bottom of this problem as he studied the hearts of people in the first Great Awakening. He helps us beware of how the gospel can bring forth thanks that has no moral worth.[1]

> True gratitude or thankfulness to God for his kindness to us, arises from a foundation laid before, of love to God for what he is in himself; whereas a natural gratitude has no such antecedent foundation. The gracious stirrings of grateful affection to God, for kindness received, always are from a stock of love already in the heart, established in the first place on other grounds, viz. God's own excellency.[2]

In other words, gratitude that is pleasing to God is not first a delight in the benefits God gives (though that will be part of it). True gratitude must be rooted in something else that comes first—namely, a delight in the beauty and excellency of God's character. If this is not the foundation of our gratitude, then it is not above what the "natural man," apart from the Spirit and the new nature in Christ, experiences. In that case "gratitude" to God is no more

---

[1] The following thoughts are based on what I wrote about "How Not to Commit Idolatry in Giving Thanks," in *A Godward Life, Book One* (Sisters, Ore.: Multnomah, 1997), 213-214.
[2] Jonathan Edwards, *Religious Affections*, in *The Works of Jonathan Edwards*, vol. 2, ed. John Smith (New Haven, Conn.: Yale University Press, 1959), 247.

pleasing to God than all the other emotions that unbelievers have without delighting in him.

You would not be honored if I thanked you often for your gifts to me but had no deep and spontaneous regard for you as a person. You would feel insulted, no matter how much I thanked you for your gifts. If your character and personality do not attract me or give me joy in being around you, then you will just feel used, like a tool or a machine to produce the things I really love.

So it is with God. If we are not captured by his personality and character, displayed in his saving work, then all our declarations of thanksgiving are like the gratitude of a wife to a husband for the money she gets from him to use in her affair with another man.

CAN GRATITUDE FOR THE CROSS BE IDOLATROUS?

It is amazing that this same idolatry is sometimes even true when people thank God for sending Christ to die for them. Perhaps you have heard people say how thankful we should be for the death of Christ because it shows how much value God puts upon us. In other words, they are thankful for the cross as an echo of our worth. What is the foundation of this gratitude?

Jonathan Edwards calls it the gratitude of hypocrites. Why? Because "they first rejoice, and are elevated with the fact that they are made much of by God; and then on that ground, [God] seems in a sort, lovely to them. . . . They are pleased in the highest degree, in hearing how much God and Christ make of them. So that their joy is really a joy in themselves, and not in God."[3] It is a shocking thing to learn that one of today's most common descriptions of the cross—namely, how much of our value it celebrates—may well be a description of natural self-love with no spiritual value.

Oh, that we would all heed the wisdom of Jonathan Edwards here. He is simply spelling out what it means to do all things—including giving thanks—to the glory of God (1 Cor. 10:31). He is showing us what the gospel is for. It is for the glory of God. And

---

[3] Ibid., 250-251.

God is not glorified if the foundation of our gratitude for the gospel is the worth of its gifts and not the value of the Giver. If gratitude for the gospel is not rooted in the glory of God beneath the gift of God, it is disguised idolatry. May God grant us a heart to see in the gospel the light of the glory of God in the face of Christ. May he grant us to delight in him for who he is, so that all our gratitude for his gifts will be the echo of our joy in the excellency of the Giver!

WHY GOD CREATED A MATERIAL WORLD

This is my answer to a hundred questions about the good things that God has made and given. The creation of the material world, including our bodies with all five senses, was God's idea. He did not do it mainly as a temptation to idolatry, but mainly as a display of his glory. "The heavens declare the glory of God" (Ps. 19:1). That is the purpose of a million species of animals and plants, and a million galaxies. "Everything created by God is good, and nothing is to be rejected if it is received with thanksgiving" (1 Tim. 4:4). Yes, if the thanksgiving is rooted in the sight of the glory of the Giver who is more to be admired *than* all his gifts, and supremely to be enjoyed *in* all his gifts.

I would love to say more about this here—the role of the creation in mediating glory from, and worship to, the Creator. But I have devoted significant space to this in a chapter titled "How to Wield the World in the Fight for Joy" in *When I Don't Desire God: How to Fight for Joy.*[4] I hope you will go there, if you desire to go deeper into this issue.

Suffice it to say here that God created what is not God. Therefore it is good that what is not God exists. The reason that God created what is not God is that this was the best way for God to display his glory to beings other than himself. His motive in this was simultaneously a love for *them* and for the *display* of his glory. I say "simultaneously" because these two things happen

---

[4] John Piper, *When I Don't Desire God: How to Fight for Joy* (Wheaton, Ill.: Crossway Books, 2004), 175-206.

in the same act. God is revealed, and we are loved. Love gives us what is best for us, and what is best for us is knowing and enjoying God. He knows best how to make the fullness of his glory known for our enjoyment. It was not without the material creation. He accomplished love for us and the display of himself by creating the material world. This continues to happen as God gives us eyes to see that all of creation "declares the glory of God."

THE GLORY OF GOD IN THE GOSPEL EXCEEDS ALL HIS GLORY IN NATURE

Moreover, God went beyond the revelation of his glory in nature and in man by working redemptively in the material world *after* the fall. This was not just to recover for man the lost vision of God, but to reveal in the gospel vastly more of his glory than could have ever been known without the fall and the history of redemption.

John Owen had a keen insight into the unique revelation of the glory of God in the gospel. This was where he riveted his attention as he prepared to die and meet Christ face to face.

> The revelation made of Christ in the blessed Gospel is far more excellent, more glorious, and more filled with rays of divine wisdom and goodness, than the whole creation and the just comprehension of it, if attainable, can contain or afford. Without the knowledge hereof, the mind of man, however priding itself in other inventions and discoveries, is wrapped up in darkness and confusion.[5]

Thus in the gospel, as with creation—only more than in creation—God's love for us and his revelation of himself happen in the same act. The highest act of love is the giving of the best gift, and, if necessary, at the greatest cost, to the least deserving. This is what God did. At the cost of his Son's life, to the totally undeserving, God gave the best gift—the display of the glory of Christ who

---

[5] John Owen, *Meditations and Discourses on the Glory of Christ in His Person, Office, and Grace*, in *The Works of John Owen*, vol. 1 (Edinburgh: Banner of Truth, 1965), 275.

is the image of God. None of this would have been possible without the created material world.

WE USE THE WORLD FOR FEASTING AND FASTING

Therefore we must not look on the material world as evil. It is fraught with temptation in this age. But the solution to that is not retreat from the world. That is impossible. We always take our sinful heart with us. The embattled pathway to heaven is a biblically balanced yes and no to the world God has made. The Christian discipline of fasting and the Christian privilege of feasting mark the route for this pathway. Here is the way I tried to capture the delight and the danger of the material world in *A Hunger for God.*

Why did God create bread and design human beings to need it for life? He could have created life that has no need of food. He is God. He could have done it any way he pleased. Why bread? And why hunger and thirst? My answer is very simple: He created bread so that we would have some idea of what the Son of God is like when he says, "I am the bread of life" (John 6:35). And he created the rhythm of thirst and satisfaction so that we would have some idea of what faith in Christ is like when Jesus said, "He who believes in me shall never thirst" (John 6:35). God did not have to create beings who need food and water, and who have capacities for pleasant tastes.

But man is not the center of the universe, God is. And everything, as Paul says, is "from him and through him and to him" (Romans 11:36). "To him" means everything exists to call attention to him and to bring admiration to him. In Colossians 1:16, Paul says more specifically that "all things were created by [Christ] and for [Christ]." Therefore bread was created for the glory of Christ. Hunger and thirst were created for the glory of Christ. And fasting was created for the glory of Christ.

Which means that bread magnifies Christ in two ways: by being eaten with gratitude for his goodness, and by being forfeited out of hunger for God himself. When we eat, we taste the emblem of our heavenly food—the Bread of Life. And when we fast we say, "I love the Reality above the emblem." In the heart of the saint both eating and fasting are worship. Both magnify Christ. Both send the heart—grateful and yearning—to the Giver. Each has its appointed place and each has its danger. The danger of eating is that we fall in love with the gift; the danger of fasting is that we belittle the gift and glory in our will-power.[6]

SEAMLESS JOY IN GOD AND HIS GIFTS

But when the gospel of Jesus Christ frees us to see and savor the glory of God above all things, the way is opened for us to experience seamless joy in God and his gifts. We are able to see every gift as a beam from the sun of God's glory. Every joy in the beam runs up to the fountain of light and ends there. No created thing becomes a rival but only a revelation of God. Therefore we can say that, for the gospel-liberated mind, all joy in created things is seamless with joy in God.

We cannot say this of the unbeliever who delights in many of the same things as the believer. We can say to the believer: your delight in your child, rightly experienced, is delight in God. A regenerate person will hear this and sense what you mean and rejoice and deepen that experience. But the unregenerate person will have no idea what you are talking about. Joy in a child is joy in a child, not God. This is a great tragedy, and one more reason why we must preach the gospel and make plain what we mean when we say, *God* is the gospel.

THE PROMISE AND PERIL OF SPIRITUAL POWER

It is inevitable in a fallen material world that tests and temptations will abound. The gospel comes with great power for salvation—to free us from everything that keeps us from seeing and savoring God above all things. Therefore power is a good gospel gift. But even power can be deceptive, and God is jealous that we not love spiritual power more than himself.

God will even use alien spiritual power to test whether he him-

---

[6] The previous two paragraphs are taken from John Piper, *A Hunger for God: Desiring God Through Prayer and Fasting* (Wheaton, Ill.: Crossway Books, 1997), 21.

self is the One we love rather than the gift of power. Consider this amazing test in Deuteronomy 13:1-3.

> *If a prophet or a dreamer of dreams arises among you and gives you a sign or a wonder, and the sign or wonder that he tells you comes to pass, and if he says, "Let us go after other gods," which you have not known, "and let us serve them," you shall not listen to the words of that prophet or that dreamer of dreams. For the LORD your God is testing you, to know whether you love the LORD your God with all your heart and with all your soul.*

In other words, it is not only the material world that tempts us to love the gift above the giver. The spiritual world has the same dangers. Love for signs and wonders may displace love for God just like any material thing.

This should caution us about a misplaced emphasis on miracles in leading people to Christ. It is possible to make the mistake of Simon the magician. He was entranced by Peter's supernatural power and wanted it, but was in fact "in the gall of bitterness and in the bond of iniquity" (Acts 8:23). I do not deny the proper place of miracles, even today. Luke stated it clearly in Acts 14:3, "The Lord . . . bore witness to the word of his grace, granting signs and wonders." Like all God's gifts, signs and wonders witness to the nature and character of God, especially his grace. But, as with material gifts, miraculous gifts may lure our hearts to themselves and not to God. This is why we must keep emphasizing that God is the gospel.

THE DEADLY LINK BETWEEN SPIRITUAL POWER AND PHYSICAL PLEASURE

Jesus showed how closely connected material pleasures are to spiritual signs of power. After Jesus fed the five thousand with five barley loaves and two fish, the crowds came looking for Jesus. But Jesus did not see true discipleship in their hearts. He said, "Truly, truly, I say to you, you are seeking me, not because you saw signs, but because you ate your fill of the loaves" (John 6:26). In other words, they missed the point of the miracle. The point was to help them see the majesty of

Christ and worship him. But what they saw was a mere miracle. And they really believed in the miracle. But that kind of belief is no honor to Christ. The devil believed in the miracle too, and he trembled. The people believed, and they wanted to put it to use for their merely natural purposes. The gospel does not offer an add-on to natural life. It offers the all-satisfying glory of God in the face of Christ.

All the enticements to God that are not God are precious and precarious. They can lead us to God or lure us to themselves. They may be food or marriage or church or miracles. All of these blessings bring love letters from God. But unless we stress continually that God himself is the gospel, people will fall in love with the mailman—whether his name is forgiveness of sins or eternal life or heaven or ministry or miracles or family or food.

WE DROVE A STAKE IN THE GROUND AT OUR WEDDING: GOD ABOVE ALL

There are some spectacular statements in the Bible to protect us from this mistake. One of my favorites—partly because it was read at our wedding in 1968—is Habakkuk 3:17-18. "Though the fig tree should not blossom, nor fruit be on the vines, the produce of the olive fail and the fields yield no food, the flock be cut off from the fold and there be no herd in the stalls, yet I will rejoice in the LORD; I will take joy in the God of my salvation." What could be clearer here than that God himself is more precious than life and all the earthly good that life gives? The aim of this book is to show that the greatest good that was purchased and promised through the gospel is the experience of knowing and enjoying God in Jesus Christ like that.

THE LOVE OF GOD, WHICH SUSTAINS LIFE, IS BETTER THAN LIFE

David said the same thing in Psalm 63:1-3.

> *O God, you are my God; earnestly I seek you; my soul thirsts for you; my flesh faints for you, as in a dry and weary land where there is no water. So I have looked upon you in the sanctuary, beholding*

*your power and glory. Because your steadfast love is better than life,
my lips will praise you.*

What is most remarkable is that he says, "Your steadfast love is
better than life." The reason that is so remarkable is that this very
"steadfast love" is repeatedly celebrated in Psalms because it rescues
and protects and preserves and defeats the enemy. It is the root of a
hundred earthly blessings. But when David ponders all the earthly gifts
of the steadfast love of God, he says that the love itself is "better than
life"—the life where all these earthly gifts are enjoyed. I take this to
mean that the God who loves him is better than all the gifts of his love.

"THERE IS NOTHING I DESIRE BESIDES YOU"

This is the mind-set of the psalmist Asaph when he prays these
radically God-exalting words: "You guide me with your counsel, and
afterward you will receive me to glory. Whom have I in heaven but
you? And there is nothing on earth that I desire besides you. My flesh
and my heart may fail, but God is the strength of my heart and my
portion forever" (Ps. 73:24-26). There is nothing in heaven or on earth
that I desire besides you, O God. That must mean, first, that if every
other good thing were lost, Asaph would still rejoice in God. And it
must mean, second, that in and through all the other good things on
earth and in heaven, Asaph sees God and loves him. Everything is
desired for what it shows of God. Augustine put it like this: "He loves
Thee too little who loves anything together with Thee which he loves
not for Thy sake."[7]

Jesus put it like this: "Whoever loves father or mother more
than me is not worthy of me, and whoever loves son or daughter
more than me is not worthy of me" (Matt. 10:37). Jesus must be
the supreme treasure of our lives, if we are true disciples of Jesus.
Jesus died for us and rose again to make it possible for us to see
him and savor him above all things with everlasting joy. This is the
great good the gospel is meant to accomplish.

---

[7] Quoted from St. Augustine, *The Confessions of St. Augustine* (X, 40), in *Documents of the
Christian Church*, ed. Henry Bettenson (London: Oxford University Press, 1967), 54.

Therefore those who are permeated most deeply by the gospel speak like the apostle Paul: "Whatever gain I had, I counted as loss for the sake of Christ. Indeed, I count everything as loss because of the surpassing worth of knowing Christ Jesus my Lord" (Phil. 3:7-8).

GOD IS THE GREATEST GIFT OF THE GOSPEL IN AND ABOVE ALL OTHERS

What I have been trying to show in this and the previous chapters is that even though the gospel purchased and promises many good gifts, from the most spiritual to the most material, yet God himself is the ultimate good promised in the gospel. If we do not see and savor that greatest good *above* all others and *in* all others, we do not yet know why the good news is truly good. Jonathan Edwards expressed very powerfully this truth that God himself is our supreme joy and is the true and lasting joy in all other joys.

> The redeemed have all their objective good in God. God himself is the great good which they are brought to the possession and enjoyment of by redemption. He is the highest good, and the sum of all that good which Christ purchased. God is the inheritance of the saints; he is the portion of their souls. God is their wealth and treasure, their food, their life, their dwelling place, their ornament and diadem, and their everlasting honor and glory. They have none in heaven but God; he is the great good which the redeemed are received to at death, and which they are to rise to at the end of the world. The Lord God, he is the light of the heavenly Jerusalem; and is the 'river of the water of life' that runs, and the tree of life that grows, 'in the midst of the paradise of God'. The glorious excellencies and beauty of God will be what will forever entertain the minds of the saints, and the love of God will be their everlasting feast. The redeemed will indeed enjoy other things; they will enjoy the angels, and will enjoy one another: but that which they shall enjoy in the angels, or each other, or in anything else whatsoever, that will yield them delight and happiness, will be what will be seen of God in them.[8]

[8] Jonathan Edwards, "God Glorified in the Work of Redemption, by the Greatness of Man's Dependence upon Him, in the Whole of It (1731)" (sermon on 1 Corinthians 1:29-31), in *The Sermons of Jonathan Edwards: A Reader*, ed. Wilson H. Kimnach, Kenneth P. Minkema, and Douglas A. Sweeney (New Haven, Conn.: Yale University Press, 1999), 74-75.

Father, I desire that they also, whom
you have given me, may be with me where I am,
to see my glory that you have given me because
you loved me before the foundation of the world.
O righteous Father, even though the world does
not know you, I know you, and these know that
you have sent me. I made known to them your
name, and I will continue to make it known,
that the love with which you have loved me
may be in them, and I in them.

JOHN 17:24-26

11

THE GOSPEL—WHAT MAKES IT ULTIMATELY GOOD: SEEING GLORY OR BEING GLORIOUS?

The best news of the Christian gospel is that the supremely glorious Creator of the universe has acted in Jesus Christ's death and resurrection to remove every obstacle between us and himself so that we may find everlasting joy in seeing and savoring his infinite beauty. The saving love of God is his doing whatever must be done, at great cost to himself, and for the least deserving, so that he might enthrall them with what will make them supremely happy forever, namely, himself. Therefore, the gospel of God and the love of God are expressed finally and fully in God's gift of himself for our everlasting pleasure.[1] "In your presence there is fullness of joy; at your right hand are pleasures forevermore" (Ps. 16:11)

---

[1] For some serious reflections on the relationship between the two halves of the answer to the first question of the Westminster Catechism ("Man's chief end is to glorify God and enjoy him forever") see Benjamin B. Warfield, "The First Question of the Westminster Shorter Catechism," in *The Westminster Assembly and Its Work*, in *The Works of Benjamin B. Warfield*, vol. 6 (reprint, Grand Rapids, Michigan: Baker, 2003), 379-400.

CHRIST IS A SOUL-SATISFYING PORTION

Those who have seen God most clearly in the face of Christ and have savored him most fully tell us something of what this is like. Jonathan Edwards opens the window on his own soul and on the meaning of the gospel with these exultant words:

> They that have Christ, they have a soul-satisfying portion. They have the truest pleasures and comforts. Here is to be found the proper happiness of the soul. Least liable to accidents and change. . . . Here is the best employment for the understanding. . . . Such as have Christ, they have better and greater riches than others. . . . Better honor. . . . Far better pleasures than sensual men. The joys are more exquisitely delighting than ever was enjoyed by the greatest epicure. [There are] no pleasures like those that are by the enlightenings of the Spirit of Christ, the discoveries of the beauty of Christ and the manifestations of his love.[2]

This is why Jesus said that the pure are blessed—because "they shall see God" (Matt. 5:8). It's why David said, "One thing have I asked of the LORD, that will I seek after: that I may dwell in the house of the LORD all the days of my life, *to gaze upon the beauty of the LORD* and to inquire in his temple" (Ps. 27:4). Beholding the beauty of God has always been the supreme desire of those who know him best.

PRAISE IS TO THE EGO WHAT SEX IS TO THE BODY

The upshot of saying this is that the love of God and the gospel of God are radically God-centered. God loves us by giving us himself to enjoy. The gospel is good news because it announces to us that God has acted in Christ not just that we may have heaven, but so that we may have God. "Everyone who . . . does not abide in the teaching of Christ, *does not have God*" (2 John 9). The greatest good of the gospel is "having God" as our treasure forever.

---

[2] Jonathan Edwards, "Glorying in the Savior," in *Sermons and Discourses 1723-1729*, in *The Works of Jonathan Edwards*, vol. 14, ed. Kenneth P. Minkema (New Haven, Conn.: Yale University Press, 1997), 467.

The God-centered love of God is foreign to fallen human beings, especially those who, like most of us, have been saturated for decades with doctrines of self-esteem. We have absorbed a definition of love that makes *us* the center. That is, we feel loved when someone makes much of us. Thus the natural, human definition of love is making much of someone. The main reason this feels like love is that it feels so good to be made much of. The problem is that this feels good on wholly natural grounds. There is nothing spiritual about it. No change in us is needed at all to experience this kind of "love." This love is wholly natural. It operates on the principles that are already present in our fallen, sinful, and spiritually dead souls. We love the praise of man. It feels good. Praise is to the ego what sex is to the body. It just doesn't get any better—as long as we are spiritually dead.

The ground of natural love is finally me, not God. If you make much of me, I feel loved, because I am the final ground of my happiness. God is not in that place. He should be, but he is not. That is what it means to be unconverted and natural. The deepest foundation of my happiness is me.

WHEN UNCONVERTED PEOPLE GET RELIGION

The astonishing thing is that people in that condition can become religious without being converted. That is, they join churches and start reading the Bible and doing religious things, with no change in the foundation of their happiness. It is still themselves. They are the ground of their joy. Being made much of is the definition of love that they bring with them into the church. Therefore what feeds the need to be made much of is felt to be loving. Some churches are so misguided in their theology, they actually nurture that need and call it love. They interpret all the good feelings in the church as coming from the grace of God, when in fact natural principles can account for most of it.

Other churches may not nurture the craving to be made much of, but unconverted people may interpret everything that is happening through that lens. So when the love of God is preached, they hear it to mean simply that God makes much of us. They may even have a strong affection for God as long as they see him as the endorsement of their delight in being the foundation of their own happiness. If God can be seen as the enabler of their self-exaltation, they will be happy to do some God-exaltation. If God is man-centered, they are willing to be, in a sense, God-centered.

HOW HYPOCRITES REJOICE IN GOD

None of this is spiritual. It is purely natural. God has been reinterpreted to fit the fallen categories of human selfishness. This is hard to spot, because man is capable of many good deeds while in the glow of human praise. In other words, whole systems of imitation Christianity can be built on distorted images of the love of God and the gospel of God. Jonathan Edwards learned this to his own heartache as he studied the permutations of hypocrisy in the fall-out of the Great Awakening. I referred briefly to this insight in the previous chapter, but here is a larger quote:

> This is . . . the . . . difference between the joy of the hypocrite, and the joy of the true saint. The [hypocrite] rejoices in himself; self is the first foundation of his joy: the [true saint] rejoices in God. . . . True saints have their minds, in the first place, inexpressibly pleased and delighted with the sweet ideas of the glorious and amiable nature of the things of God. And this is the spring of all their delights, and the cream of all their pleasures. . . . But the dependence of the affections of hypocrites is in a contrary order: *they first rejoice . . . that they are made so much of by God; and then on that ground, he seems in a sort, lovely to them.*[3]

So it is possible even to see God as "in a sort, lovely" when we are not even genuine Christians. If he can be seen as a servant of our self-love, then we can see him as lovely. If he will make much of us, then we will be willing, up to a point, to make much of him.

---

[3] Jonathan Edwards, *Religious Affections*, in *The Works of Jonathan Edwards*, vol. 2, ed. John Smith (New Haven, Conn.: Yale University Press, 1959), 249-250. Emphasis added.

GOD DOES IN A SENSE MAKE MUCH OF US

We will see later in this chapter that there is a sense in which God does indeed make much of his people. But the difference is that for unconverted persons, it is precisely God's making much of them that is the *ground* of their joy. The issue is not merely whether God may approve or even praise his people (which he does). The issue is: Where does the foundation of our joy lie? What is the bottom of our happiness? Is it ourselves or is it God?

CONVERSION: THE MERCIFUL DESTRUCTION OF INFERIOR JOY

Christian conversion is the spiritual awakening of our souls to the glory of God as the ground of our joy. Conversion is the spiritual discovery that being loved by God is not the divine endorsement of our passion for self-exaltation. In fact, being loved by God is the merciful destruction of that passion. And the destruction is not an end in itself. It is to make room for the supernatural experience of truly being loved by God—that is, being enabled by him to enjoy God-exaltation as an end in itself. Spiritual God-exaltation is not a means to the pleasure of self-exaltation.

Being loved by God is the wonderful replacement of self as the foundation for our joy. In the place of self comes the glory of God. Most people know that the greatest experiences of joy in this life—the ones that come closest to being pictures of perfect joy in heaven—are not experiences of self-affirmation, but of self-forgetfulness in the presence of something majestic. Those moments are few in this life. Most of the time our joy in some splendor outside ourselves is contaminated by self-awareness and the craving of our ego to have some share in the wonder.

But we have tasted enough of self-forgetting joy to help us know what being loved by God really means. God's best gift is not the gift of self-esteem. God's best gift is God—for our everlasting and ever-increasing enjoyment. Being loved by God is the exhilarating deliverance from the hall of mirrors we once thought would bring us happiness—if we could just like what we see. Heaven is not a hall of mirrors. Or maybe we should say, heaven is a world in which all created things have become mirrors, and all of them are tilted to a 45 degree angle. Everywhere we look—in every creature—we see the reflection of God.

GOD USES TEXTS TO LIFT THE VEIL

But it seems that the man-centered definition of divine love has gone so deep, many simply cannot see it another way. Indeed, it is impossible to see until Christ lifts the veil and we are able to see the glory of God as our greatest treasure. Then it not only makes sense that his love would be the gift of himself, but we experience it.

God uses means to lift the veil, and one of those means is Scripture. It will be helpful, therefore, to focus our attention on several texts that are especially suited for showing the glory of God as the best gift of God's love. I have found that several texts in the Gospel of John help lift the veil on God's God-centered love. One of these texts is the story of Lazarus' sickness and death.

> Now a certain man was ill, Lazarus of Bethany, the village of Mary and her sister Martha. It was Mary who anointed the Lord with ointment and wiped his feet with her hair, whose brother Lazarus was ill. So the sisters sent to him, saying, "Lord, he whom you love is ill." But when Jesus heard it he said, "This illness does not lead to death. It is for the glory of God, so that the Son of God may be glorified through it." Now Jesus loved Martha and her sister and Lazarus. So, when he heard that Lazarus was ill, he stayed two days longer in the place where he was. (John 11:1-6)

THE STRANGE TIMING OF THE LOVE OF CHRIST

The first astonishing thing in this text is that Jesus did not depart right away so as to get there in time to heal Lazarus. "He stayed two days longer in the place where he was" (v. 6). In other words, he intentionally delayed and let Lazarus die. The second astonishing thing here is that this delay is described as the result of Jesus' love for his friends. Notice the word "so"[4] at the beginning of verse 6: "Jesus loved Martha and her sister and Lazarus. *So . . .* he stayed two days longer.*" Jesus let Lazarus die *because* he loved him and his sisters.

What makes sense of this? Jesus gave the answer in verse 4 when he told his disciples why Lazarus was sick: "This illness does not lead to death. *It is for the glory of God, so that the Son of God may be glorified* through it.*" Jesus had a plan. He would let Lazarus die so that he could raise him from the dead. This was a costly plan. Lazarus would have to go through the torments of death, and his family would endure four days of grieving over his death.

But Jesus considers the cost worth it. His explanation has two parts. First, in letting Lazarus die in order to raise him from the dead his aim is to show the glory of God the Father and God the Son. Second, in this costly revelation of his glory he would be loving this family. From this I conclude that the primary way that Jesus loved this family was by doing what he must do to display to them in a compelling way his own glory.

THE UNINTELLIGIBLE LOVE OF CHRIST

Many today would call Jesus callous and unloving for letting Lazarus die. And they would add this criticism: that he is vain and self-conceited if he was motivated by a desire to display his own glory. What this shows is how far above the glory of God most people value pain-free lives. For most people, love is whatever puts human value and human well-being at the highest point. So to call Jesus' behavior loving is unintelligible to them.

But let us learn from Jesus what love is and what our true well-being is. *Love is doing whatever you need to do to help people see and savor the glory of God in Christ forever and ever.* Love keeps God central. Imitating Jesus in this does not mean that we love

---

[4] The NIV ignores the universal meaning of οὖν as "therefore" or "so" and casts the verse as an adversative instead of an inference by translating it as "yet": "*Yet* when he heard that Lazarus was sick . . ." D. A. Carson observes, "The NIV's rendering of the opening of v. 6 is without linguistic defense. . . The two-day delay was motivated by Jesus' love for Martha, Mary and Lazarus." *The Gospel of John* (Grand Rapids, Mich.: Eerdmans, 1991), 407.

by seeking to display *our* glory. Imitation means that we seek to display *his* glory. Jesus sought the glory of himself and his Father. We should seek the glory of Jesus and his Father. Jesus is the one being in the universe for whom self-exaltation is the highest virtue and the most loving act. He is God. Therefore the best gift he can give is the revelation of himself. We are not God. Therefore it is not loving for us to point people to ourselves as the ground of their joy. That would be an unloving distraction. Love means helping people see and savor Christ forever.

How Christ Loves Us with Christ-Exalting Prayer

Jesus confirms that we are on the right track here by praying for us in John 17 that God would glorify him, and that we would see his glory. I am assuming that when Jesus prays for us, which he said he was doing ("[I pray] for those who will believe in me through their word," v. 20), he is loving us. His prayer is an act of love. Therefore, in accord with what we saw in John 11 he prays, "Father . . . glorify your Son that the Son may glorify you. . . . Now, Father, glorify me in your own presence with the glory that I had with you before the world existed" (vv. 1, 5).

Strange as it seems, his love for us spills over in a prayer that he himself be glorified. But it is not strange to those whose veil of man-centeredness has been lifted. This is the very glory for which we were made. Seeing the glory of God in Christ is the highest gift and the greatest pleasure we are capable of. Giving us this is what love is.

In 17:24 Jesus makes it clear that he prays for his own glory so that we would be able to see his glory. "Father, I desire that they also, whom you have given me, may be with me where I am, *to see my glory*." The reason he prayed for his glory in verse 1 was so that he could pray in verse 24 that we would be able to see it. The love of Jesus drives him to pray for us, and then die for us, not that *our* value may be central, but that *his glory* may be central, and so that we may see it and savor it for all eternity. This is the greatest good in the good news of the gospel. "Father, I desire that they . . .

be with me . . . *to see my glory."* That is what it means for Jesus to love us. Divine love labors and suffers to enthrall us with what is infinitely and eternally satisfying: God in Christ.[5]

THE UNFAIR DICHOTOMY

The question we should ask ourselves as we glory in the gospel, and as we revel in the love of God, is this: Do we feel loved by God because God makes much of us or because God, at great cost to himself, did all that needed to be done through Jesus Christ so that we might enjoy making much of him forever? It is a telling question.

But it is also a slightly unfair question, if the language is taken strictly and not in the spirit of all that's in this chapter. What's unfair is that it hangs you on a dichotomy between two choices that may not be mutually exclusive.[6] Both may be true. I admitted this earlier. There is a sense in which God *does* make much of us. That's not in dispute. What I am pleading for is that this fact is not the ultimate foundation of our joy. If not, then how does it figure into the good news of the gospel? Answering that question will lead us to our final reflections on the meaning of glorification and whether *being* like Christ or *seeing* the glory of Christ is the ultimate good of the good news.

HOW HAS GOD MADE MUCH OF US?

The way God has made much of us is by creating us in his image and calling this creation "very good." Then, after the fall, he pursues the restoration of that fallen image. But he goes beyond restoration to a new level of transformation, namely, conformity to the incarnate Son of God. "Just as we have borne the image of the man of dust, we shall also bear the image of the man of heaven" (1 Cor. 15:49). Our transformation into Christ's image proceeds progressively in this life

---

[5] These thoughts on John 11 and 17 were published originally in "How Strange and Wonderful Is the Love of Christ," in John Piper, *Pierced by the Word* (Sisters, Ore.: Multnomah, 2003), 13-15.
[6] My friend and colleague of more than twenty-five years, Tom Steller, should get credit for pressing this home to me and helping me write the rest of this chapter the way I did. What I have written would not be as biblically balanced without Tom's helpful input.

and is perfected at the resurrection. The glory of God that we obtain in this way results in our receiving praise from God.

There are clear biblical pointers to this remarkable dignity that God freely and graciously bestows on us in spite of our sinfulness. "God created man in his own image, in the image of God he created him; male and female he created them. . . . And God saw everything that he had made, and behold, it was very good" (Gen. 1:27, 31). Then, in our conversion to Christ, God starts over again, as it were: "If anyone is in Christ, he is a new creation" (2 Cor. 5:17). "We are his workmanship, created in Christ Jesus for good works" (Eph. 2:10). "[We] have put on the new self, which is being renewed in knowledge after the image of its creator" (Col. 3:10).

The aim of God's creative work in his people is to conform us to the image of Christ. "Those whom he foreknew he also predestined to be conformed to the image of his Son" (Rom. 8:29). "And we all, with unveiled face, beholding the glory of the Lord, are being transformed into the same image from one degree of glory to another" (2 Cor. 3:18).

This conformity to Christ means that we share in the glory of God—both spiritually and physically. It includes our bodies. When Christ comes again he "will transform our lowly body to be like his glorious body" (Phil. 3:21). Paul calls what will happen to us "glorification": "Those whom he predestined he also called, and those whom he called he also justified, and those whom he justified he also *glorified*" (Romans 8:30). The glory will be intolerably bright, and we will need new eyes to look on each other with pleasure, because "the righteous will shine like the sun in the kingdom of their Father" (Matt. 13:43).

We will be like a bride prepared for her immaculate husband: "Christ loved the church and gave himself up for her, that he might sanctify her . . . so that he might present the church to himself in splendor, without spot or wrinkle or any such thing, that she might be holy and without blemish" (Eph. 5:25-27). This glorification of Christ's bride—God's children—will be so central to what happens in the new creation that Paul says the rest of creation will obtain its transformation from ours: "The creation itself will be set free from its bondage to decay and obtain the freedom of the glory of the children of God" (Rom. 8:21).

The upshot of this amazing transformation will be that God himself will look upon us with delight and praise. "The LORD your God is in your midst . . . he will rejoice over you with gladness; he will quiet you by his love; he will exult over you with loud singing" (Zeph. 3:17). Peter says that the tested and refined faith of believers will "be found to result in praise and glory and honor at the revelation of Jesus Christ" (1 Pet. 1:7). And Paul says of the true Christian, "His praise is not from man but from God" (Rom. 2:29), and at the judgment "each one will receive his commendation [or: praise] from God" (1 Cor. 4:5). Knowing this, Paul tells us that "by patience in well-doing [we should] seek for glory and honor and immortality" (Rom. 2:7). And Paul says of the Thessalonians that because of what God has done in their lives through his ministry, they will be his "hope" and "joy" and "crown of boasting before our Lord Jesus at his coming" (1 Thess. 2:19).

WE WILL SEE GLORY, AND WE WILL BE GLORIOUS

In this sense, then, we may speak of God making much of us. We will see the beauty of God, and we will reflect the beauty of God. We will *see* glory, and we will *be* glorious. Jonathan Edwards put it like this:

> How happy is that love in which there is an eternal progress in all these things, wherein *new beauties are continually discovered*, and more and more loveliness, and in which *we shall forever increase in beauty ourselves*. When we shall be made capable of finding out, and giving, and shall receive more and more endearing expressions of love forever, our union will become more close and communion more intimate.[7]

[7] Jonathan Edwards, *The "Miscellanies,"* in *The Works of Jonathan Edwards*, vol. 13, ed. Thomas A. Schaefer (New Haven, Conn.: Yale University Press, 1994), 336-337 (Miscellany #198).

Both seeing and being will increase forever: "New beauties are continually discovered" in God, and "we shall forever increase in beauty ourselves." A finite mind cannot fully know an infinite mind. Our finite capacities for pleasure cannot fully know all the joy there is to be had in an infinite fountain. Therefore, the age to come will be an eternal increase of learning and loving.[8] This means that the truth of 2 Corinthians 3:18 never ceases. "Beholding the glory of the Lord, [we] are being transformed into the same image from one degree of glory to another." The better we see him, the better we will reflect him—to all eternity.

WE MUST BE LIKE CHRIST IN ORDER TO SEE THE FULLNESS OF HIS GLORY

The final question then is this: Is the greatest good purchased and promised in the gospel becoming like the glorious Christ or seeing the glory of Christ? That is, how does Romans 8:29 ("predestined to be conformed to the image of his Son") relate to John 17:24 ("Father, I desire that they also, whom you have given me, may be with me where I am, to see my glory")?

There is a clue in Romans 8:29 and its connection with Colossians 1:18. Paul says, "Those whom [God] foreknew he also predestined to be conformed to the image of his Son" (Rom. 8:29). What is the significance of Paul saying "... *in order that he might be the first-born among many* brothers"? The word "firstborn" ($\pi\rho\omega\tau\acute{o}\tau o\kappa o\nu$) is important. It is used again in Colossians 1:18, "He is the beginning, the *firstborn* [$\pi\rho\omega\tau\acute{o}\tau o\kappa o\varsigma$] from the dead, *that in everything he might be preeminent.*" In the most ultimate sense, Christ died and rose from the dead as the firstborn of many brothers so that he would be seen and enjoyed as preeminent, superior, gloriously great.

In other words, our destiny to be like Christ is ultimately about

---

[8] "If there be any change, it will be from its increase; because of better intellectual perception and knowledge of God, and of divine things; because of a constantly and increasingly endearing communion with God in Christ; because of an increased capacity to behold the glory of Christ; and because of a greater exaltation of the spiritual nation in the worship and service of the Lord." James Petigru Boyce, *Abstract of Systematic Theology* (1887; reprint, Escondido, Calif.: Dulk Christian Foundation, n.d.), 475-476.

being prepared and enabled to see and savor the glory of his superiority. We must have his character and likeness in order to know him and see him and love him and admire him the way we ought. By adding the words, "in order that he might be the *firstborn* among many brothers," Paul makes plain that Christ is ever and always supreme above his brothers. We become like him not merely to be his brothers—which is true and wonderful—but mainly to have a nature that is fully able to be in awe of him as the one who has "first place in everything" (Col. 1:18, NASB).

Without words like those at the end of Romans 8:29 and Colossians 1:18, how easily we would slip into a man-centered view of human transformation. We would tend to make our likeness to Christ the ultimate goal of the gospel. It is a goal. A glorious goal. But it is not the ultimate goal. Seeing and savoring and showing the supremacy of Christ is the ultimate goal.

A PERSONAL TEST FOR WHAT IS ULTIMATE IN OUR HEARTS

We should test ourselves with some questions. It is right to pursue likeness to Christ. But the question is, why? What is the root of our motivation? Consider some attributes of Christ that we might pursue, and ask these questions:

- Do I want to be *strong* like Christ, so I will be admired as strong, or so that I can defeat every adversary that would entice me to settle for any pleasure less than admiring the strongest person in the universe, Christ?
- Do I want to be *wise* like Christ, so I will be admired as wise and intelligent, or so that I can discern and admire the One who is most truly wise?
- Do I want to be *holy* like Christ, so that I can be admired as holy, or so that I can be free from all unholy inhibitions that keep me from seeing and savoring the holiness of Christ?
- Do I want to be *loving* like Christ, so that I will be admired as a loving person, or so that I will enjoy extending to others, even in sufferings, the all-satisfying love of Christ?

The question is not whether we will have all this glorious likeness to Christ. We will. The question is: To what end? Everything in Romans 8:29-30—all of God's work, his choosing us, predestining us, calling us, justifying us, bringing us to final glory—is designed by God not *ultimately* to make much of us, but to free us and fit us to enjoy seeing and making much of Christ forever.

NOT FINALLY BEING AND SEEING, BUT DELIGHTING AND DISPLAYING

Perhaps we have not posed the question in the best way. In asking whether *seeing* God or *being* like God is the greatest good of the gospel, we may have stopped short of what being and seeing are for. Perhaps neither is ultimate. Would it not be better to say that the ultimate benefit of the gospel, which makes all its other parts good news, is neither being nor seeing, but *delighting* and *displaying*—that is, delighting in and displaying "the glory of God in the face of Jesus Christ" (2 Cor. 4:6). In other words, is it not the case that we *behold* and thus *become* (2 Cor. 3:18; 1 John 3:2), and that we *become* and thus *behold* (Matt. 5:8; 2 Cor. 4:6) in order that ultimately we might *delight in* and *display* God? Becoming and beholding are a means to the end of delighting and displaying.

Jesus points in this direction by the way he finishes his prayer in John 17. In verse 24 he prays that we may be with him where he is, to see his glory. The emphasis falls on the great gospel gift of seeing the divine glory. But the final statement of Jesus' prayer in verse 26 is a promise that calls attention to the delight we will take in seeing this glory: "I made known to them your name, and I will continue to make it known, *that the love with which you have loved me may be in them*, and I in them."

This is an awesome promise. He is not merely saying that we will see his glory, but that when we see him, we will love him with the very love that the Father has for the Son—". . . *that the love with which you have loved me may be in them.*" This is a love that consists of supreme delight. The Father has infinite joy in the glory of his Son. We are promised a share in that joy. This means that seeing and being, by themselves, are not the ultimate benefit of the gospel. Seeing leads to *savoring* or it is not good news at all.

THE DISPLAYING OF GOD'S GLORY WILL BE SPIRITUAL AND PHYSICAL

And then, by means of this savoring or delighting in the glory of God, comes the *displaying*. It happens internally and externally. Internally, the affection of delight itself magnifies the worth of God as our supreme treasure. God is glorified in us when we are satisfied in him. Externally, Christ-exalting *deeds* flow from this enjoyment of Christ. Everything we said in the previous chapter about the importance of the material creation becomes crucial at this point. All creation, but especially redeemed humankind, will visibly and materially reflect and display the glory of God. It will be spiritual and physical. Both the Christ-exalting joy of our heart and the Christ-exalting deeds of our resurrection bodies will make known the glory of God.[9]

How then should we speak of our future *being* and *seeing* if they are not the ultimate gift of the gospel? How shall we speak of being "partakers of God's nature" (2 Pet. 1:4) and being "conformed to . . . his Son" (Rom. 8:29) and beholding his glory (John 17:24)? How shall we finally talk of being made much of by God?

---

[9] Jonathan Edwards described the relationship between pleasurable physical perceptions, on the one hand, and the spiritual delights in God, on the other hand, in the age to come after we have our resurrection bodies: "This pleasure from external perception will, in a sense, have God for its object, it will be in a sight of Christ's external glory, and it will be so ordered in its degree and circumstances as to be wholly and absolutely subservient to a spiritual sight of that divine spiritual glory, of which this will be a semblance, as eternal representation, and subservient to the superior spiritual delights of the saints. This is as the body will in all respects be a spiritual body, and subservient to the happiness of the spirit, and there will be no tendency to, or danger of, inordinacy, or predominance. This visible glory will be subservient to a sense of spiritual glory, as the music of God's praises is to the holy sense and pleasure of the mind, and more immediately so, because this that will be seen by the bodily eye will be God's glory, but that music will not be so immediately God's harmony." *The "Miscellanies," in The Works of Jonathan Edwards*, vol. 18, ed. Ava Chamberlain (New Haven, Conn.: Yale University Press, 2000), 351.

AN ENDLESS WAVE OF INCREASING REVELATION OF DIVINE GLORY

Woe to us if we speak of our existence, or our being, for its own sake. God has given us existence. It is a great wonder, full of trembling and awe. We exist by him, through him, and for him (Rom. 11:36). The ultimate and greatest good of the gospel is not self-admiration or self-exaltation, but *being* able to see the glory of God without disintegrating, and *being* able to delight in the glory of Christ with the very delight of God the Father for his own Son, and *being* able to do visible Christ-exalting deeds that flow from this delight. So *being* like God is the ground of *seeing* God for who he is, and this seeing is the ground of *savoring and delighting in* the glory of God with the very delight of God, which then overflows with *visible displays* of God's glory.

In this way the gospel of God reaches its final goal in a universal and corporate reality, not just an individual one. A wave of revelation of divine glory in the saints and in creation is set in motion that goes on and on and grows for all eternity. As each of us sees Christ and delights in Christ with the delight of the Father, mediated by the Spirit, we will overflow with visible actions of love and creativity on the new earth. In this way we will see the revelation of God's glory in each other's lives in ever new ways. New dimensions of the riches of the glory of God in Christ will shine forth every day from our new delights and new deeds. And these in turn will become new ways of showing and seeing Christ that will elicit new delights and new doings. And so the ever-growing wave of the revelation of the riches of the glory of God will roll on forever and ever. And it will be made plain that the great and final good of the gospel is God.[10]

---

[10] These final thoughts are also found in slightly different form in the forthcoming book *Contending for Our All* (Wheaton, Ill.: Crossway Books, 2006). I owe a debt to St. Athanasius for stirring up these thoughts, and I try to pay the debt in the chapter called "Contending for Christ *Contra Mundum*: Exile and Incarnation in the Life of Athanasius."

For his sake I have suffered the loss of all things
and count them as rubbish in order that
I may gain Christ.

PHILIPPIANS 3 : 8 B

My soul longs, yes, faints for the courts
of the LORD; my heart and flesh sing for you
to the living God.

PSALM 84 : 2

Be Thou my Vision, O Lord of my heart;
Naught be all else to me, save that Thou art
Thou my best Thought, by day or by night,
Waking or sleeping, Thy presence my light.

DALLAN FORGAILL

CONCLUSION:
GOD IS THE GOSPEL—
NOW LET US SACRIFICE
AND SING

IT IS NOT LOVE IF IT DOESN'T GIVE GOD

God loves as no other being can or should love. No one else in the universe can or should love by giving us the gift of himself. I don't mean that a human being cannot lay down his life for others and call it love. I mean no human being can lay down his life for others *in order that others might treasure him*, and call it love. It would not be love. It would be a distraction—and in relation to God, treason.

I am not an all-satisfying treasure. Therefore, if I live or die in order that you may have *me* as your treasure, I cheat you and deflect your heart from God, your everlasting joy. If I would love you, I must do what Jesus did. I must live and die to give you God. That's what Jesus did. That's what God does. God's highest act of love is giving us himself to love.

To say it yet another way, love labors and, if need be, suffers to enthrall us with what is supremely and eternally satisfying, namely, God. This is true for Christ's love, and it is true for our love. Christ loves by suffering to give us God. We love by suffering to give God to others. Giving ourselves without giving God looks loving to the world. But it is not. We are a poor substitute for God. We are not the nobler because we die for them, if our hearts have no longing that our death lead them to God. One of the radical implications of this book is that if we would love like Christ, we will bear whatever pains it takes to make Christ's glory seen. The aim of love—whether by gospel word or giving up our life—is to enthrall the beloved with the glory of Christ in the face of God forever.

THE INDISPENSABLE, LITERAL, FACTUAL, HISTORICAL CORE OF THE GOSPEL

Thus we have seen that the highest, best, and final good that makes the gospel good news is the glory of Christ who is the image of God (2 Cor. 4:4). Seeing and savoring and displaying this—without any sin, and with the mighty aid of the Spirit—is the final joy promised in the gospel. Nothing else in the gospel is good news unless it leads to this—the enjoyment of the glory of God in Christ. The death and resurrection of Jesus Christ for our sins are the indispensable, once-for-all, historical deeds of the gospel (1 Cor. 15:3-4). There is no gospel without their literal, factual, historical reality.

But these events are only good news because of what they bring about. Standing alone in history without effect, they would be no news at all, let alone good news. They are good news because by the death and resurrection of Christ the propitiation of God's wrath and the forgiveness of our sins and the imputation of Christ's righteousness become ours by faith alone. God's anger is removed from him, our guilt is removed from us, Christ's obedience is counted as ours—this is the effect of Christ being crucified in our place and raised from the dead.

Too many Christians stop here in answering the question, what is the gospel? Too many think they have said what makes the good news good when they have only spoken of God's wrath removed and guilt taken away and righteousness imputed. But why are propitiation and forgiveness and imputation good news? What makes them good news? The answer to this question, and whether it is given with joy, makes all the difference in the world.

THE FINAL GOOD THAT MAKES THE GOOD NEWS GOOD IS GOD

Even if one answers that these truths are good news because they provide escape from hell and entrance to heaven, what have we learned from that answer? We have not learned the decisive thing. We have not learned why a person wants to go to heaven. Oh, how many there are for whom heaven represents merely the absence of pain and the presence of eternal happiness! But now comes the absolutely decisive question: Is this happiness in God himself or in the gifts of heaven?

The point of this book is that the Christian gospel is not merely that Jesus died and rose again; and not merely that these events appease God's wrath, forgive sin, and justify sinners; and not merely that this redemption gets us out of hell and into heaven; but that they bring us to the glory of God in the face of Jesus Christ as our supreme, all-satisfying, and everlasting treasure. "Christ . . . suffered once for sins, the righteous for the unrighteous, *that he might bring us to God*" (1 Pet. 3:18).

GOD IS THE GOSPEL

That is what I mean by the title *God Is the Gospel*. And lest there be any misunderstanding, let it be clear that from this final point of God-centered joy in the glory of God, the goodness and joy of God's glory stream back through the gift of heaven and the work of justification and forgiveness and propitiation and resurrection and crucifixion. And the effect is that now these central gospel events and effects shine all the more brightly with what makes them truly good news—the revelation of the glory of God in the face of Christ.

Now when we herald the death and resurrection of Jesus as good news, we are not just exulting in God's acts or God's gifts. We are showing the final joyful reason for calling them *good* news. When we proclaim that the death and resurrection of Jesus is the ground for propitiating God's wrath and forgiving sin and imputing righteousness, we are not just assuaging guilt and relieving fears—we are displaying the glory of God. We are making known not merely divine acts and divine gifts—we are making known the truth and beauty and worth of Christ himself who is the image of God. By God's sovereign, creative power, we are opening the eyes of the blind (Acts 26:17b-18; 2 Cor. 4:4, 6) to see in the gospel "the light of the knowledge of the glory of God in the face of Jesus Christ." We are making plain that there is no salvation through the gospel where the best and highest and final good in the gospel is not seen and savored. That good is the glory, the worth, the beauty, the treasure of Christ himself who is true God and true man.

THE TRANSFORMING POWER OF THE GLORY OF CHRIST IN THE GOSPEL

Now when we pursue sanctification—the fight for holiness and the fight against sin—we will fight by means of the gospel perhaps differently than we ever have. In our own struggles, and in our counseling, and (for some of us) in our preaching, we will realize that the power of the gospel to transform us into radically loving people lies not only in our being forgiven and our being counted righteous, but also in our seeing and savoring the glory of Christ in the gospel.

We will elevate 2 Corinthians 3:18 to a place of paramount importance in our practical pursuit of love and justice. "And we all, with unveiled face, beholding the glory of the Lord [in the gospel], are being transformed into the same image from one degree of glory to another." In other words, the fight to become like Christ will be, as never before, a fight to see and savor Jesus Christ. When, for example, we try to help a teenage boy triumph over pornography, we will work and pray to help him see and savor the glory of Christ. We will not merely use accountability structures and filters and human reasonings. We will seek to saturate his mind and heart with the enthralling vision of the all-satisfying Christ. We will not assume it is easy. We will remember that the god of this world wants to blind our minds from seeing the light of the gospel of the glory of Christ (2 Cor. 4:4). But now we know where the battle is mainly to be fought. It is fought at the level of spiritual sight. This is the path of gospel freedom and radical Christ-like love.[1]

NOW LET US PRAY AND SACRIFICE AND SING

We have come to the end of the book. How shall we take our leave of each other? Perhaps with the pledge of prayer and a word of exhortation. Make it your aim from now on to see the glory of Christ in the gospel. Make it your aim to let the eyes of your heart run up the beam of glory shining in the gospel until your mind's attention and your heart's affection rest in God himself. And when, by this vision, you have been freed from the vanities of this world, then give yourself to the highest, humblest, and happiest calling in the world—the display of the glory of Christ in the declaration and demonstration of gospel love. To this end I pledge my prayers for you.

Perhaps there is one last service I could render. Though we now see in a mirror dimly what we will one day witness face to face, still we have seen enough to know that we must sing. There is no part of the gospel that should not be sung. Every facet in the diamond is a spark that has ignited fire in the soul of Christian poets who have put their pen to paper for the sake of the church. But the glory of the whole diamond shines with one great brightness—namely, Jesus Christ, the image of God. Therefore, to help you sing of this, I gather here some songs that over the centuries have celebrated Christ as our supreme treasure.

FOURTEEN CENTURIES OF SONGS THAT
SAVOR CHRIST

Originally composed in Old Irish, the words of "Be Thou My Vision" are attributed to the eighth-century Irish poet, Dallan Forgaill. If the church of Jesus Christ today around the world prayed

---

[1] See "The Fight for Joy Is a Fight to See," in John Piper, *When I Don't Desire God: How to Fight for Joy* (Wheaton, Ill.: Crossway Books, 2004), 57-69.

this prayer steadfastly and wholeheartedly, what a Copernican revolution of God-centeredness would likely come to pass!

> *Be Thou my Vision, O Lord of my heart;*
> *Naught be all else to me, save that Thou art;*
> *Thou my best Thought, by day or by night,*
> *Waking or sleeping, Thy presence my light.*
>
> *Be Thou my Wisdom, and Thou my true Word;*
> *I ever with Thee and Thou with me, Lord;*
> *Thou my great Father, I Thy true son;*
> *Thou in me dwelling, and I with Thee one.*
>
> *Be Thou my battle Shield, Sword for the fight;*
> *Be Thou my Dignity, Thou my Delight;*
> *Thou my soul's Shelter, Thou my high Tower:*
> *Raise Thou me heavenward, O Power of my power.*
>
> *Riches I heed not, nor man's empty praise,*
> *Thou mine Inheritance, now and always:*
> *Thou and Thou only, first in my heart,*
> *High King of Heaven, my Treasure Thou art.*
>
> *High King of Heaven, my victory won,*
> *May I reach Heaven's joys, O bright Heaven's Sun!*
> *Heart of my own heart, whatever befall,*
> *Still be my Vision, O Ruler of all.*

Four hundred years later in the twelfth century the French mystic Bernard of Clairvaux wrote in Latin "Jesus, the Very Thought of Thee." One of the blessings of songs like this is to build a vocabulary of delight into our minds even as the affection of spiritual pleasure is wakened in our hearts by the contemplation of Christ.

> *Jesus, the very thought of Thee*
> *With sweetness fills the breast;*
> *But sweeter far Thy face to see,*
> *And in Thy presence rest.*

Nor voice can sing, nor heart can frame,
Nor can the memory find,
A sweeter sound than Thy blest Name,
O Savior of mankind!

O hope of every contrite heart,
O joy of all the meek,
To those who fall, how kind Thou art!
How good to those who seek!

But what to those who find? Ah, this
Nor tongue nor pen can show;
The love of Jesus, what it is,
None but His loved ones know.

Jesus, our only joy be Thou,
As Thou our prize wilt be;
Jesus be Thou our glory now,
And through eternity.

O Jesus, light of all below,
Thou fount of living fire,
Surpassing all the joys we know,
And all we can desire.

The Christ-saturated saints of every age have sounded the note that the world's best bliss cannot compare to the pleasures of faith in the presence of Christ. The superior joy of knowing Jesus is the theme of Bernard's "Jesus, Thou Joy of Loving Hearts."

Jesus, Thou Joy of loving hearts,
Thou Fount of life, Thou Light of men,
From the best bliss that earth imparts,
We turn unfilled to Thee again.

Thy truth unchanged hath ever stood;
Thou savest those that on Thee call;
To them that seek Thee Thou art good,
To them that find Thee all in all.

We taste Thee, O Thou living Bread,
And long to feast upon Thee still;
We drink of Thee, the Fountainhead,
And thirst our souls from Thee to fill.

Our restless spirits yearn for Thee,
Wherever our changeful lot is cast;
Glad when Thy gracious smile we see,
Blessed when our faith can hold Thee fast.

O Jesus, ever with us stay,
Make all our moments calm and bright;
Chase the dark night of sin away,
Shed over the world Thy holy light.

One of the most well-known hymns in the English language was written by an unknown person in German as *Schönster Herr Jesu* in the seventeenth century. It was first published in the *Münster Gesangbuch* in 1677 and was translated into English by Joseph A. Seiss in 1873. "Fairest Lord Jesus" takes seriously all the beauties of nature and affirms at every turn that Christ is more beautiful. The fourth verse is usually omitted in the hymnbooks but expresses one truth that the others do not—namely, that Jesus is not only fairer than all the beauties of nature, but is also the sum of all beauty. What we see in nature we see even more gloriously in Christ.

Fairest Lord Jesus, Ruler of all nature,
O Thou of God and man the Son,
Thee will I cherish, Thee will I honor,
Thou, my soul's glory, joy and crown.

Fair are the meadows, fairer still the woodlands,
Robed in the blooming garb of spring;
Jesus is fairer, Jesus is purer,
Who makes the woeful heart to sing.

Fair is the sunshine, fairer still the moonlight,
And all the twinkling starry host;

Jesus shines brighter, Jesus shines purer
Than all the angels heaven can boast.

All fairest beauty, heavenly and earthly,
Wondrously, Jesus, is found in Thee;
None can be nearer, fairer or dearer,
Than Thou, my Savior, art to me.

Beautiful Savior! Lord of all the nations!
Son of God and Son of Man!
Glory and honor, praise, adoration,
Now and forever more be Thine.

Georg Michael Pfefferkorn, a teacher and pastor, also wrote in German. His hymn, *Was frag' ich nach der Welt*, published in 1667, was translated into English in 1923 by August Crull as "What Is the World to Me?" Though it is not well-known, it does express the many ways that Christ surpasses all that the world can offer.

What is the world to me,
With all its vaunted pleasure
When Thou, and Thou alone,
Lord Jesus, art my Treasure!
Thou only, dearest Lord,
My soul's Delight shalt be;
Thou art my Peace, my Rest—
What is the world to me?

The world is like a cloud
And like a vapor fleeting,
A shadow that declines,
Swift to its end retreating.
My Jesus doth abide,
Though all things fade and flee;
My everlasting Rock—
What is the world to me?

The world seeks after wealth
And all that Mammon offers,

Yet never is content
Though gold should fill its coffers.
I have a higher good,
Content with it I'll be:
My Jesus is my Wealth—
What is the world to me?

The world is sorely grieved
Whenever it is slighted
Or when its hollow fame
And honor have been blighted.
Christ, Thy reproach I bear
Long as it pleaseth Thee;
I'm honored by my Lord—
What is the world to me?

The world with wanton pride
Exalts its sinful pleasures
And for them foolishly
Gives up the heavenly treasures.
Let others love the world
With all its vanity;
I love the Lord, my God—
What is the world to me?

The world abideth not;
Lo, like a flash 'twill vanish;
With all its gorgeous pomp
Pale death it cannot banish;
Its riches pass away,
And all its joys must flee;
But Jesus doth abide—
What is the world to me?

What is the world to me?
My Jesus is my Treasure,
My Life, my Health, my Wealth,
My Friend, my Love, my Pleasure,
My Joy, my Crown, my All,

My Bliss eternally.
Once more, then, I declare—
What is the world to me?

One could take a hymn like this too far and discount all the gifts of God as having no Christ-exalting value. That would be a mistake. Should we take the risk of singing this way? Yes, because of the biblical precedent in even more radical texts like Psalm 73:25, "Whom have I in heaven but you? And there is nothing on earth that I desire besides you." And 16:2, "I say to the Lord, 'You are my Lord; I have no good apart from you.'" And Philippians 3:8, "I count everything as loss because of the surpassing worth of knowing Christ Jesus my Lord." Sometimes the heart sees the surpassing worth of God in such stark contrast to all that he has made, the best way to say it is that God is all and the rest is as nothing. I hope I have protected us from unbiblical world-denunciation in Chapter 10.

Johann Franck joins the chorus of his remarkable century in Germany and sings of Jesus as the source of purest pleasure. "Jesu, meine Freude" was published in 1653 and was translated from German into English by Catherine Winkworth in 1863 as "Jesus, Priceless Treasure."

Jesus, priceless Treasure, Source of purest pleasure,
Truest Friend to me, long my heart hath panted,
'Til it well nigh fainted, thirsting after Thee.
Thine I am, O spotless Lamb,
I will suffer naught to hide Thee, ask for naught beside Thee.

In Thine arms I rest me; foes who would molest me
Cannot reach me here. Though the earth be shaking,
Every heart be quaking, Jesus calms our fear.
Sin and hell in conflict fell,
With their heaviest storms assail us, Jesus will not fail us.

Hence, all thought of sadness! For the Lord of gladness,
Jesus, enters in. Those who love the Father,
Though the storms may gather, still have peace within;

Yea, whate'er we here must bear,
Still in Thee lies purest pleasure, Jesus,
priceless Treasure!

Charles A. Tindley was born in 1851. As the son of an American slave he taught himself to read and earned his divinity degree by correspondence. "In 1902, he became pastor of the Calvary Methodist Episcopal Church in Philadelphia, Pennsylvania, the church where he had earlier been the janitor. At the time of Tindley's death, his church had 12,500 members. . . . Tindley's 'I'll Overcome Some Day' was the basis for the American civil rights anthem 'We Shall Overcome.'"[2] "Nothing Between My Soul and My Savior" was written in 1905. In the gospel genre it represents the passion of a lover of Christ never to allow any competing pleasure to come between the soul and the Savior.

Nothing between my soul and my Savior,
Naught of this world's delusive dream;
I have renounced all sinful pleasure;
Jesus is mine, there's nothing between.

Nothing between, like worldly pleasure;
Habits of life, though harmless they seem;
Must not my heart from Him ever sever;
He is my all, there's nothing between.

Nothing between, like pride or station;
Self or friends shall not intervene;
Though it may cost me much tribulation,
I am resolved, there's nothing between.

Nothing between, e'en many hard trials,
Though the whole world against me convene;
Watching with prayer and much self denial,
I'll triumph at last, there's nothing between.

---

[2] Quoted from http://www.cyberhymnal.org/bio/t/i/tindley_ca.htm, accessed on 5-4-05.

The twentieth century saw an explosion of popular worship music. Surprisingly, much of it was riveted on Christ and his redemptive work. I say surprisingly because the lyrics of these songs far surpassed the preaching of those days in God-centeredness and manifest affection for the exalted Christ. "Knowing You"[3] by Graham Kendrick is a retelling of Philippians 3:7-12. The song, especially the refrain, weaves together the preciousness of Jesus himself with the great gospel truth of Christ's imputed righteousness.

> *All I once held dear, built my life upon*
> *All this world reveres, and wars to own*
> *All I once thought gain I have counted loss*
> *Spent and worthless now, compared to this*

> *Knowing you, Jesus, knowing you,*
> *There is no greater thing.*
> *You're my all, you're the best,*
> *You're my joy, my righteousness,*
> *And I love you, Lord.*

> *Now my heart's desire is to know you more,*
> *To be found in you and known as yours,*
> *To possess by faith what I could not earn*
> *All-surpassing gift of righteousness*

> *Oh, to know the power of your risen life,*
> *And to know you in your sufferings;*
> *To become like you in your death, my Lord,*
> *So with you to live and never die.*

At the beginning of the twenty-first century there has been, at least in some groups, an increasing focus on the central work of Christ on the cross. One of the best musical expressions of what *God Is the Gospel* has been trying to say is "I Will Glory in My

---

[3] Graham Kendrick , "Knowing You," Copyright © 1993 Make Way Music, P.O. Box 263, Croydon, Surrey. CR9 5AP, U.K.

Redeemer"[4] by Steve and Vikki Cook. Its narration of gospel events, with their effects, is powerful: Christ's blood ransomed me—the Lamb is my righteousness—he crushed the power of sin and death—my life he bought—he carries me on eagles' wings—he waits for me at gates of gold.

Yet the sixfold repetition of the line, "I will glory in my Redeemer" leaves no room for doubt: the point of all the gospel events and gospel effects is to enthrall us with Christ himself. Both now and in the final day Christ is all. "I have no longings for another / I'm satisfied in Him alone." So it will be in the hour of death: "And when He calls me it will be paradise / His face forever to behold."

Why will it be paradise to behold the face of Christ forever? Because this is the gospel—seeing and savoring "the light of the knowledge of the glory of God in the face of Jesus Christ" (2 Cor. 4:6). God, shining in the face of Christ, for our everlasting and ever-increasing joy, is the best and highest and final good that makes the good news good.

> *I will glory in my Redeemer*
> *Whose priceless blood has ransomed me*
> *Mine was the sin that drove the bitter nails*
> *And hung Him on that judgment tree*
> *I will glory in my Redeemer*
> *Who crushed the power of sin and death*
> *My only Savior before the holy Judge*
> *The Lamb Who is my righteousness*
> *The Lamb Who is my righteousness*
>
> *I will glory in my Redeemer*
> *My life He bought, my love He owns*
> *I have no longings for another*
> *I'm satisfied in Him alone*
> *I will glory in my Redeemer*

[4] Music and lyrics by Steve & Vikki Cook. © 2001 PDI Worship (ASCAP). Sovereign Grace Music, a division of Sovereign Grace Ministries. From *Upward: The Bob Kauflin Hymns Project*.

His faithfulness my standing place
Though foes are mighty and rush upon me
My feet are firm, held by His grace
My feet are firm, held by His grace

I will glory in my Redeemer
Who carries me on eagles' wings
He crowns my life with loving-kindness
His triumph song I'll ever sing
I will glory in my Redeemer
Who waits for me at gates of gold
And when He calls me it will be paradise
His face forever to behold
His face forever to behold

To which I sing, Amen.

✸ desiringGod

If you would like to further explore the vision of God and life presented in this book, we at Desiring God would love to serve you. We have hundreds of resources to help you grow in your passion for Jesus Christ and help you spread that passion to others. At our website, desiringGod.org, you'll find almost everything John Piper has written and preached, including more than thirty books. We've made over twenty-five years of his sermons available free online for you to read, listen to, download, and in some cases watch.

In addition, you can access hundreds of articles, find out where John Piper is speaking, learn about our conferences, discover our God-centered children's curricula, and browse our online store. John Piper receives no royalties from the books he writes and no compensation from Desiring God. The funds are all reinvested into our gospel-spreading efforts. Desiring God also has a whatever-you-can-afford policy, designed for individuals with limited discretionary funds. If you'd like more information about this policy, please contact us at the address or phone number below. We exist to help you treasure Jesus Christ and his gospel above all things because he is most glorified in you when you are most satisfied in him. Let us know how we can serve you!

Desiring God
Post Office Box 2901 Minneapolis, Minnesota 55402
888.346.4700   mail@desiringGod.org

SCRIPTURE INDEX

PERSON INDEX

Subject Index